SHARPEN YOUR

SUPERVISION

Other titles in this series

Sharpen your skills in motivating people to perform
Trevor Bentley 007 709072 1

Sharpen your team's skills in effective selling
Trevor Bentley   007 709279 1

Sharpen your team's skills in developing strategy
Susan Clayton   007 709281 3

Sharpen your team's skills in creativity
Trevor Bentley   007 709282 1

Sharpen your team's skills in coaching
Tony Voss   007 709278 3

Sharpen your team's skills in project management
Jean Harris   007 709140 X

Sharpen your team's skills in people skills
Di Kamp   007 709276 7

Sharpen your team's skills in time management
Jane Allan   007 709275 9

SHARPEN YOUR TEAM'S SKILLS IN

S UPERVISION

Susan Clayton

The McGraw-Hill Companies

London · New York · St Louis · San Francisco · Auckland · Bogotá · Caracas
Lisbon · Madrid · Mexico · Milan · Montreal · New Delhi · Panama · Paris
San Juan · São Paulo · Singapore · Sydney · Tokyo · Toronto

Published by
McGraw-Hill Publishing Company
Shoppenhangers Road, Maidenhead, Berkshire, SL6 2QL, England
Telephone 01628 502500
Facsimile 01628 770224

British Library Cataloguing in Publication Data
Clayton, Susan
  Sharpen your team's skills in supervision
  1. Supervisors – Training of   2. Supervision of employees
  I. Title   II. Supervision
  658.3'02

  ISBN 0-07-709280-5

Library of Congress Cataloging-in-Publication Data
Clayton, Susan
    Sharpen your team's skills in supervision / Susan Clayton.
      p.   cm.
    ISBN 0-07-709280-5 (pbk. : alk. paper)
    1. Supervisors–Training of.   2. Supervisors–Training of–
  Problems, exercises, etc.   I. Title.
  HF5549.15.C58   1996
  658.4'071244–dc20   96-34950
                                                             CIP

McGraw-Hill

A Division of The **McGraw·Hill** Companies

Based on an original work by Bobette Hayes Williamson: *The ASTD
Trainer's Sourcebook: Supervision* (0 07 053437 3) McGraw-Hill New York
1996

12345 CUP 99876

Typeset by BookEns Ltd, Royston, Herts
Printed and bound in Great Britain at the University Press, Cambridge

Printed on permanent paper in compliance with ISO Standard 9706

CONTENTS

EXERCISES

Series Preface

This series of books focuses on helping you to improve the performance of your team by providing a range of training and support materials. These materials can be used in a variety of ways to improve the knowledge and skills of your team.

The creation of high performance is achieved by paying attention to three key elements:

- The skills or competencies of your people
- The way these skills are applied
- The support your people receive from you in applying their skills.

SKILL DEVELOPMENT

The books in this series will provide materials for the development of a range of skills on a subject-by-subject basis. Each book will provide information and exercises in manageable chunks which will be presented in a format that will allow you to choose the most appropriate way to deliver them to your staff. The contents will consist of all you need to guide your staff to a full understanding of the subject.

There are at least four ways you could choose to guide the learning of your team; these are:

- Training sessions
- Learning groups
- Open learning
- Experiential learning.

TRAINING SESSIONS

These can be run by bringing your people together and

guiding them step by step through the materials, including the exercises. During these sessions you can invite your people to interact with you and the materials by asking questions and relating the materials to their current work. The materials will provide you with the detailed information you need to present the subject to your team.

LEARNING GROUPS

This approach involves dividing your team into small groups of two, three or four people and having a brief session with each group in which you introduce them to the materials. Each group then works through the materials and meets with you from time to time to assess progress and receive your guidance.

OPEN LEARNING

This approach invites your people to use the materials at their own speed and in their own way. This is a form of individual learning which can be managed by regular meetings between you and your team as individuals or in a group. The process is started by introducing the materials to your team and agreeing some *learning outcomes* to be achieved.

EXPERIENTIAL LEARNING

This calls for you to invite your team to examine the materials using the exercises as a focus, and then to get them to relate what they are learning directly to real-life situations in the workplace. This experience of the learning is then shared and discussed by the team as a whole.

The books in the series have been designed to enable these four approaches to be used, as well as other ways that you might think are more appropriate to your team's specific needs.

APPLYING SKILLS

Time spent developing skills can be wasted if people do not have the opportunity to practise them. It is important that you consider this aspect of performance before embarking on a particular programme. It is useful if you are able to clearly identify opportunities for practising skills and discuss these with your team. Providing opportunities for practising and further developing competency is part and parcel of the whole approach of this series.

PROVIDING SUPPORT

Once people have acquired a new skill and have been provided with opportunities to apply it, they still need your support and coaching while they are experimenting with using it. The opening book in this series, *Sharpen your skills in motivating people to perform*, provides clear guidance on how to help people to develop their skills and then how to provide experience, practice and support as they use these skills.

Before starting work with your team on the materials in this book I suggest you do the following:

1. Review the materials yourself
2. Plan the approach you are going to follow
3. Discuss with your team what you are planning
4. Agree some learning outcomes
5. Indicate how you are going to support your team during the learning process.

The authors in the series have endeavoured to provide a range of materials that is comprehensive and will support you and your team. I hope that during this process you learn from and enjoy the experience.

Dr Trevor J. Bentley
Series Editor

ABOUT THE EDITORIAL PANEL

Dr Trevor Bentley, series editor for this series, is a freelance organizational consultant, a facilitator and a writer. Prior to becoming a consultant and while working as a senior executive, Trevor carried out a major research project into decision making and organization structures for which he was awarded his PhD. Over the last 20 years he has had a wide range of experience working with organizations in over 20 countries. Trevor has trained for four years with Gestalt South West and attended Gestalt workshops in the UK and Europe. He now applies a Gestalt approach in his work.

Trevor has written 20 books and over 250 articles on business-related issues. His background includes careers as a management accountant, financial director, computer systems designer, management services manager, human computer interface consultant, trainer and business manager. His current area of interest is in the application of a Gestalt approach to solving problems of organizational harmony. This includes culture change, performance management, team facilitation, executive coaching, mentoring and integrated supervision.

Mike Taylor is a consultant involved in the design, implementation and facilitation of personal and team development programmes within organizations. After graduating in 1987, he worked with two outdoor management training providers, both as a manager and tutor. His work has a strong focus on the use of experiential learning in developing managers, mainly within larger organizations.

Mike also works with groups and single individuals in running meetings and events which help teams and individuals explore working practices and approaches. More recently he has developed an interest in Gestalt as a way of understanding group processes. He is a member of the Association for Management Education and Development.

Dr Tony Voss is a counsellor, consultant and trainer. He originally trained as a chemist before working in environmental research developing sea-going computer systems and information technology, and later in the computer industry as a project manager, consultant and quality manager. Tony has a particular interest in enabling people to contribute fully and creatively to their endeavours, and sees this as benefiting individuals, their organizations and society at large. He is an Accredited Counsellor with the British Association for Counselling, and he also trained in Gestalt over a four-year period.

Tony works with those wanting to develop their organization and people, and those dealing with particular challenges in their working life. His clients also include those exploring the role of work in their life, as well as those with more personal issues.

ABOUT THE AUTHOR

Susan Clayton is a leading contributor to the use and development of Gestalt philosophy and practice in organizations. Focusing on human processes, she enables managers and their staff to achieve business goals that depend on managing people. Her skill in raising awareness of how people relate to each other can forge supportive alliances and powerful cooperative relationships. Her approach includes helping people to manage blocks and difficulties in their contact with others, clearing the way for work and business relationships to move forward and grow.

Susan works with managers at all levels. Her interventions have aided groups in turmoil, managers needing to reach common agreement and individuals needing mentoring and coaching support. She helps organizations understand how to manage in a way that creates trust, respect and clarity in human relationships.

CHAPTER 1

PREPARING THE LEARNING FOR SUPERVISORS

KEY LEARNING POINT

■ **Setting up a learning programme**

Making the transition from operating employee to supervisor is challenging. It is the first step into management requiring a shift in perspective, attitude and work practices. The three basic elements for success in the supervisory role are: fitting well into the management system; developing good operational skills; and working well with people. This book provides the resource to support the learning of all three elements. A philosophy for continual improvement is woven into the learning process.

The book is divided into two parts. Part 1 helps supervisors to:

■ understand where they fit into the management system
■ identify the many different roles in their work

■ look at some key responsibilities in relation to different ways of learning.

Part 2 focuses more on skills development with a particular emphasis on planning methods, getting the best out of people, leadership and teamwork. The final chapter looks at how you, the manager, and the supervisors can develop and maintain a productive working relationship.

The approach adopted is designed to support the integration of learning in the workplace. Many exercises relate to the specific work that supervisors are engaged in, thus giving their learning relevance and substance.

SETTING UP A STRUCTURE FOR LEARNING

One of the first things you may wish to do is set up a structure for learning. The type of framework that you could adopt is shown in the following example.

Learning approach	Structure
Purpose of the training	● To train supervisors in the knowledge and skills that they need to add value to their work and to support my role as manager ● Measures of success to be agreed at the first meeting
Training sessions	● Two hours a week for 12 weeks ● Resources to cover work during training sessions to be arranged
Peer learning groups (3 to 4 in each group)	● To be set up at the first session with a clear purpose of focusing on specific aspects of supervising and for skill practice ● Peer groups agree how they will operate ● Resources to cover worktime taken out for this to be agreed

Learning approach	Structure
Mentoring support	• *To approach suitable mentors before the first meeting and establish their willingness to participate, explaining that the role is to offer extra support for the learning process* • *To link mentors with trainee supervisors at the first session*

There are many variations you could try for structuring the learning. Much will depend on the environment and circumstances in which you work. Establishing a framework to work with and remaining open to negotiate changes at the first session with your employees, will provide a clear basis from which to work.

Particular attention needs to be given to learning support; what people need to help them learn and take risks within the working conditions of the department. Without being able to take risks, and therefore chance not getting it right, the capacity to learn is reduced. Learning peer groups and mentoring systems with other skilled supervisors can ensure that good support is available.

Exercise 1 – Setting up your learning structure

Structure a learning plan similar to the example given. This learning plan should provide a clear structure for your supervisors' development needs in relation to their work. Having gained some idea of the material contained in this book, you may have a view on the essential requirements for your supervisors' specific learning needs and, therefore, material that is less relevant. This material could be introduced in different ways, for example, essential material through training sessions, less relevant material through peer learning groups.

Learning programme for supervisors ....(date)

Learning approach	Structure

CONCLUSION

People face many challenges when they take on a supervisor's role. They often take on the job having developed a good knowledge of the operational side of the business. One of the key challenges they face is in their changing relationships with staff, peers and managers. Frequently there is not a good enough support system that will help them learn and grow well into their new role, supporting them when they don't quite get it right. Above all they have to change their perspective from hands-on work to letting this go, moving into a role of supporting others to achieve individual and departmental objectives.

PART 1

*L*AYING THE FOUNDATIONS

PART 1

KEY LEARNING POINT

■ Assessing the readiness of people to become supervisors

Today the role of a supervisor is an important step into the management system. Supervision lays the foundations to achieve high performance and requires that supervisors know what this means.

The following five chapters will enable supervisors to create firm foundations for achieving high-performance supervision. **Chapter 2** describes the challenges facing supervisors, the skills that they will need to develop and a mind-set of carrying out their role in a way that adds value to the department. **Chapter 3** explores how supervisors need to fit in with the organization's management system, what high performance management looks like, and develops an understanding of working in political systems.

Chapter 4 will help supervisors to deal effectively with conflicting loyalties between their boss and their ex-peers. This is a particularly difficult area that supervisors find themselves in, especially early on in their new role. **Chapter 5** addresses the issue of the many different roles that supervisors have to take on. This can be quite an eye-opener for supervisors and helpful for them to learn how to take on different roles with confidence. **Chapter 6** looks at how supervisors can develop into their new responsibilities through building knowledge, skills and experience.

The manager's first task is selecting the right people for their supervisory roles. People who have: technical know-how and operational experience; an interest in working with people and personnel issues; a willingness to learn, develop and take risks; the potential to work within the management system. Assessing the readiness of an employee to take on a supervisory role is not always easy. For example, operational staff who have had a wide range of experience in the business and show all the signs of a good supervisor at the work face, may not be a good leader or work well in dealing with personnel problems.

The following assessment will help you and your staff to decide their readiness.

Exercise 2 – How ready are you to be a supervisor?

How ready are you to be a supervisor?

Read each statement carefully. Then place a tick in the column that most nearly matches your feeling about each statement. After completing this activity, check your answers using the scoring procedure that follows the list.

Agree	Disagree	Neither agree nor disagree		
____	____	____	1.	I like to set my own goals and do things my own way.
____	____	____	2.	I have a keen sensitivity to the interests of other people.
____	____	____	3.	I see my work as a means only to an end, rather than as a main focus for my life.
____	____	____	4.	When I know a job needs to be done well, I will do it myself.
____	____	____	5.	I don't want to take the responsibility for someone else's work, good or bad.
____	____	____	6.	I consider myself an attentive listener: I don't interrupt.
____	____	____	7.	Given a fair chance, most people want to do a good job.
____	____	____	8.	I live according to the rule of 'better late than never'.
____	____	____	9.	When working with a group of other people on a project, I often find

				myself prodding them to get the job done.
_____	_____	_____	**10.**	I have a lot to learn about management and supervision.
_____	_____	_____	**11.**	Good employees work safely, obey the rules, and are willing to give a fair day's work.
_____	_____	_____	**12.**	My friends know that I won't criticize them when they come to me with their hard-luck stories.
_____	_____	_____	**13.**	People who break rules should be prepared to pay the penalty.
_____	_____	_____	**14.**	I like to show other people how to do things.
_____	_____	_____	**15.**	The thought of working overtime without extra pay seems extremely unfair.
_____	_____	_____	**16.**	Most of my bosses have been a hindrance rather than a help to me and my co-workers.
_____	_____	_____	**17.**	I consider myself to be a good explainer: I can make things clear to other people.
_____	_____	_____	**18.**	In handling my personal affairs, I rarely fall behind in what I set out to do.
_____	_____	_____	**19.**	When assessing a situation, I find that there is likely to be some good in it as well as the bad and the ugly.
_____	_____	_____	**20.**	When things go wrong, that's a sign that a problem needs to be solved rather than a person blamed.

Source: Lester R. Bittel and John W. Newstrom, *What Every Supervisor Should Know*, Sixth Edition, New York: McGraw-Hill, 1990. Adapted and reprinted with permission.

Scoring

Give yourself one point for each of the following statements that you *agreed* with: 2, 6, 7, 9, 10, 11, 12, 13, 14, 17, 18, 19, 20. Give yourself one point for each of the following statements that you *disagreed* with: 1, 3, 4, 5, 8, 15, 16. There are no points for statements with which you neither agreed nor disagreed.

	Agree		Disagree
2.	_____	1.	_____
6.	_____	3.	_____
7.	_____	4.	_____
9.	_____	5.	_____
10.	_____	8.	_____
11.	_____	15.	_____
12.	_____	16.	_____
13.	_____		
14.	_____		
17.	_____		
18.	_____		
19.	_____		
20.	_____		
Total	_____		_____

Interpretation

If you scored between 15 and 20 points, you are ready to consider the pursuit of a supervisory position. If you scored between 9 and 14 points, you should try now to gain a fuller understanding of what a supervisory position entails. If you scored less than 9 points, it's probably wise to look to other occupations for a career. Do continue your studies of supervision, however, so that your working life will be made more fruitful from your understanding of the supervisors and managers with whom you will be associated.

CHAPTER 2

BECOMING A SUPERVISOR

KEY LEARNING POINTS
- Understand the challenges facing new supervisors today
- Understand the concept of value-added supervision
- Skills assessment for supervisors

OVERVIEW OF SUPERVISION

HIGH-PERFORMANCE SUPERVISION

Supervisors are at the forefront of operations, interacting moment by moment with employees to accomplish the work of the business. Each day the supervisor's job becomes more challenging as the business strives to maintain the high performance levels essential to survival in a fiercely competitive global economy.

High–performance supervision pulls diverse contributors together into a cohesive team, committed to achieving the organization's vision, while at the same time enabling each individual to perform at their personal best.

SUPERVISORS HAVE MORE RESPONSIBILITY

Today mid-level managers often have two to three times as many people reporting to them than they might have had in the past. For instance, a manager who formerly had eight first-line supervisors could have 20 or more in a downsized organization. Also, the manager has more paperwork and less clerical support. Consequently they have less time to spend directing the work of first-line supervisors. As a result, first-line supervisors are acting more independently and taking on more responsibility.

SUPERVISORS ARE DEVELOPING POLICIES AND STRATEGIES

Instead of carrying out orders formulated at the executive level and relayed by middle management, first-line supervisors and their work teams are becoming more involved in developing policies and strategies. They are creating process, product and service innovations. Additionally, first-line supervisors are working collaboratively across organizational lines for the overall good of the business. In a cascade effect, some operational workers are handling jobs previously done by the first-line supervisor, such as scheduling work hours and holidays, and taking responsibility for process and quality control for their areas.

ORGANIZING, INFLUENCING AND PROBLEM-SOLVING SKILLS ARE INCREASINGLY IMPORTANT

Faced with heavier work loads and more complex responsibilities, supervisors are redefining which tasks are critical, and delegating more work to capable employees. They are resisting the temptation to take over when an employee has a problem. Instead, supervisors are building employee skills through coaching. As organizations become less hierarchical and more fluid, supervisors are sharpening their influence skills so they can work collaboratively with peers, upper management cross-functional teams, suppliers and customers.

VALUE-ADDED SUPERVISION

Supervisors are expected to add value to the business in

Supervisors are expected to
add value to the business in
tangible ways

tangible ways. Simply passing information up and down the chain or directing employees to perform tasks is not enough. Supervisors can add value by:

- Identifying value-added steps and non–value-added steps in processes or operations, and improving the process. A test question is: Would customers be willing to pay for the steps if they knew you were performing them?
- Scrutinizing indirect costs.
- Initiating new projects that have value.
- Connecting the right people with the right information.
- Learning continuously and applying the knowledge.
- Encouraging employees to learn continuously and to apply their knowledge.
- Adding value to information by interpreting it or building on it.
- Adding to the organization's knowledge base; for example, streamlining a process after analysing customer feedback and then sharing the innovation with other work units.
- Redesigning work to take advantage of changing technology.
- Building the organization's 'memory' by adding knowledge to shared electronic databases.

Exercise 3 – Value-added supervision

Discuss with your supervisors the concept of value-added supervision. It is enough for them to learn the language at this stage rather than go too deeply into what it means in their work.

The following short exercises will help open up the discussion:

- Ask your supervisors to identify people in management and supervisory roles in your organization who appear to operate through a 'value-added' philosophy.
- Get your supervisors to identify specific behaviours that demonstrate the value-added approach in people around them.
- Ask each supervisor what they might already do that adds value to their work.

■ Explore what added value they think customers would be willing to pay for in their work as a supervisor.

THE SKILLS OF A SUPERVISOR

Managers at every level are involved in contributing to the business through planning ahead and bringing out the best in their staff in order to achieve their objectives. What differs at each management level is the focus managers take as they perform their functions. For instance, top management take a long-term strategic focus, middle management an intermediate focus and first-line supervisors a near-term operational focus. These principles apply to any organization: profit and non-profit, public sector and private, small and large, manufacturing and service.

PLANNING AHEAD

Planning ahead is a process of envisioning the future, setting goals, identifying actions to achieve the goals, establishing target dates for completing the actions and describing measures for success. A plan is a written document and provides the basis for putting tasks into action and for reviewing them.

SKILLS FOR BRINGING LIFE INTO THE FRAME

In spite of technology developments and automation which have radically changed work structures and practices, business does not exist without people. Not only do people bring skills and expertise to perform tasks and functions, of equal importance is that they bring a tapestry of colour – through their personalities, their individuality, differences and their values and beliefs. This is what gives a business spirit. The role of the supervisor is to keep this spirit alive for this is what ultimately contributes to high performance levels and added value. It is people that put life into the business.

People bring a tapestry of colour through their individuality

MANAGING PERFORMANCE

Managing performance involves setting standards and measuring performance against those standards. Setting goals and objectives, giving feedback to staff and encouraging a philosophy and practice of continuous improvement forms a large part of a supervisor's responsibilities in this area.

PEOPLE SKILLS

Getting the best out of people requires skills in coaching and training, setting goals and objectives, working in teams, and a flexible, influential style of leadership. Good inter-personal skills and an engaging communication style will help. Above all, perhaps the most essential people skill of a supervisor is to listen.

LEADERSHIP

Leading is the process of influencing other people to follow in the achievement of a common goal. To lead effectively, supervisors must make positive use of power. Power is the ability to influence the behaviour of others and is found in two different dimensions: personal power and positional power.

To lead effectively, supervisors must make positive use of power

While the business vests positional power in the supervisor, employees recognize personal power of their supervisor because they respect and like him or her, or because they see the value that their supervisor brings to the work of the department.

Characteristics that enhance the supervisor's power include a clear vision, sense of mission, energy, strength of character, the ability to motivate and communicate, persuasiveness, self-confidence, courage, competence, integrity, honesty and their personality.

GETTING THE BEST OUT OF TEAMS

Working well with teams takes a special sort of skill and is often quite difficult for new supervisors to develop. Working collaboratively, instead of being too directive or controlling, can be highly productive and involving. Getting the best out of teams requires that team members work well together, building on the differences that they bring. The team leader plays a very significant part in engendering this.

Some team skills that supervisors will need to have are:

- *To be able to nurture creativity and inspire innovation*   Help to sell the team's innovative ideas.
- *To preserve the team's knowledge base*   Ensure that the knowledge base developed within the department is documented and added to electronic databases, so others can benefit from and build upon the learning.
- *To provide opportunities for team visibility*   Give teams opportunities to gain visibility and to share their learning, for example by giving briefings.
- *To keep focused on strategic vision*   Help teams keep projects aligned with the organization's strategic vision.
- *To keep teams well-informed*   Bring teams together periodically for progress updates and discussions of critical issues.
- *To offer practical guidance*   Guide teams in problem-solving, decision-making and conflict resolution processes.

Chapter 15 'Working together' specifically looks at the manager–supervisor relationship.

WORKING WELL WITH THE MANAGER

It goes without saying that a good working relationship between manager and supervisor has a positive impact on operational staff. This is a relationship that has to be worked on, it cannot be assumed that it will simply fall into place. The responsibility of ensuring good relations falls with both manager and supervisor.

Exercise 4 – Assessing supervisory skills

All of us are naturals at some things and not so good at others. We can finely tune those things that we are good at, develop further the skills that we are not so good at and seek other people's support for tasks requiring skills that we are not interested in developing. Being aware of our range of skills helps us to manage our work more productively.

Ask your supervisors to rate themselves on the following *skill areas* based on the natural abilities and skills that they know they have.

Skill areas	Not very good	About average	Very good
Planning ahead			
Managing performance			
People skills:			
• Delegation			
• Dealing with difficult behaviours			
• Coaching and training			
• Inter-personal skills			
• Communication skills			
• Problem-solving			
• Decision-making			
Leadership			
Getting the best out of your team			
Working well with your manager			

CONCLUSION

The essence of high-performance supervision is that supervisors respect the importance of their role, in the belief that what they do has the potential to add value to the business. To supervise well they need to integrate the skills for operational functions with people skills. Understanding their starting point, what they are good at and not so good at, creates a framework for their future learning and success.

CHAPTER 3

FITTING IN WITH MANAGEMENT

KEY LEARNING POINTS

- Understand how supervision fits into the organization's management system
- Know the difference between high-performance and low-performance supervision
- Know how to work in a political system

THE MANAGER INSIDE

Some thoughts for you, before you meet your supervisors on this subject.

As the manager and coach for helping supervisors learn, imagine yourself coming into supervision for the first time. You may even remember the time when you first took on a supervisor's role. See if you can really step into, or step back to, that experience. Then consider the following questions:

- Could you have illustrated clearly how your role fitted into the wider management system?
- What did it feel like to be moving away from your peers towards a management role?

- What expectations did you have of your boss and the staff that you were supervising?
- What did you understand about organizational politics?

Notice what you experience as you ask yourself these questions. Then consider how you might support your supervisors if they were to raise similar questions for themselves.

Supervisors must begin to appreciate that they are a part of a much wider management and political system. That it is within this system that they achieve their own goals, which contribute to the organization's goals and overall vision. Their own success is dependent on their skills to communicate well, to influence others and to integrate into the system.

At some stage you may wish to share your response to the questions with your supervisors.

FITTING IN WITH THE MANAGEMENT SYSTEM

Supervisors occupy the first rung on the management ladder. They focus the efforts of operating staff to accomplish the goals of the organization. In control-oriented, hierarchical organizations, supervision is direct, day-to-day, hour-by-hour, hands-on management. In more participative net-worked environments supervisors may play a more diffused role as team leaders, facilitators or coaches.

THE WIDER PICTURE

Figure 3.1 shows that as people move up through the management ladder their technical expertise becomes less important and their people management begins to increase. Supervision is the first step. The need to manage people and let go of some of the hands-on operational aspects of work can often be difficult for new supervisors. Raising awareness of this difficulty with new supervisors encourages them to face the challenge and deal with it as a normal transitional experience that they can work through.

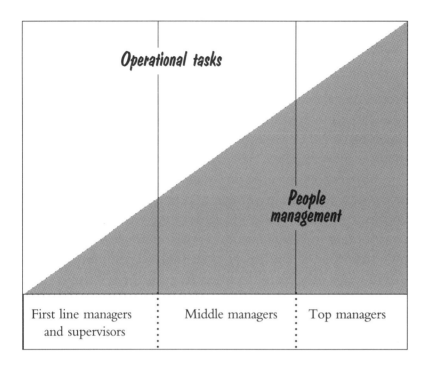

FIGURE 3.1: The balance of work between operational tasks and managing people

MANAGEMENT SYSTEMS

As Figure 3.2 shows most organizations have three broad management levels: executive or top management, middle management and first line supervisors. In large organizations each level can also have several sub-levels. In addition, there are generally two streams – line management and staff management. These streams and levels form an interconnected system of management functioning:

- *Line managers* oversee line functions, which are activities central to producing products and services: for instance, engineering, production, manufacturing, finance, marketing and sales.
- *Staff managers* support the achievements of people and their interaction with line functions: for instance, human resources, training and development, public relations, information systems and administrative services.

Essential to this role is how the supervisors' responsibilities connect with the wider functions of the business

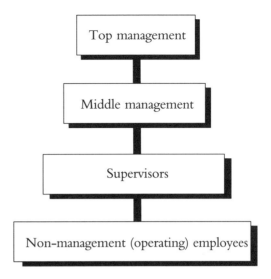

FIGURE 3.2: Management levels

TOP MANAGERS/EXECUTIVES

Taking a long-term focus the top management team anticipate and plan for the future of the business. They develop the vision, mission, strategic plan, long-term goals and policies which establish the direction of the business. Top management are also concerned with external forces such as general economic conditions, the political climate, legislation and public opinion.

MIDDLE MANAGERS

The role of middle managers is to plan and implement programmes that carry out objectives and directives set by top management. They also manage and support the work of supervisors and people who work in specialized areas. The upper layer of middle managers reports directly to top management.

SUPERVISORS

Supervisors manage and direct the daily efforts of non-managerial employees who do the hands-on work. With their staff and teams they bring the managements' vision into today's operations. Supervision is not an isolated function, it contributes to the whole of the organization system. Essential to this role is an interest in the business, the industry and how the supervisors' responsibilities connect with the wider functioning of the organization and management system.

Today supervision can range from working directly with staff and teams through daily contact, to distant supervision with home-workers. The difference lies in the way the supervisors communicate and support the people involved.

Exercise 5 – Supervising within the management system

This exercise will help supervisors understand where they are positioned within the management system and where their direct lines of communication exist.

1. Draw up a flow chart of the management system in your organization, specifically identifying the management links that directly and indirectly affect your supervisory role and responsibilities.
2. Compare your chart with what you might know or imagine about:
   - other supervisory roles in different functions within your organization.
   - other supervisory roles in competitor companies.

HIGH-PERFORMANCE VERSUS LOW-PERFORMANCE MANAGEMENT

The two lists shown in Table 3.1 contrast the healthy results of high-performance management on the part of supervisors, middle managers and executives with the costly consequences of low-performance management. Most organizations fall somewhere in the middle of the continuum. The high performers are leading-edge, world-class businesses. Those with low performance ratings are heading downhill unless they change course quickly and radically.

The attributes identified here for managers also offer supervisors an awareness of the type of outcomes they can expect from both good and bad supervision.

TABLE 3.1 Attributes of high and low performance

High-performance management	Low-performance management
● Strong commitment to shared vision	● Confusion about the business's direction. Individual goals more important than business's goals
● Information is shared widely. People communicate openly and honestly	● Information is guarded closely. Rumours abound
● Trust levels are high	● People distrust each other's motives. Political manoeuvering is common
● Excellent safety record	● High accident rates. Insurance claims result
● Employees develop professionally	● Employee skills are becoming obsolete. Recruitment and training costs are high due to turnover
● High employee morale	● Low morale. High employee stress levels, absenteeism and sickness
● People of diverse backgrounds are accepted; their ideas are valued	● Recruitment and promotions often are based on favouritism. Grievances, discrimination complaints and litigation against the company result
● Cooperative labour relations	● Strained labour relations, grievances, slow-downs and strikes
● Able to recruit and retain talented employees and board members	● Talented employees and board members leave. Difficulty recruiting replacements
● Facilities and equipment are state-of-the-art and well maintained	● Facilities and equipment are aging. Downtime and repairs are frequent
● High productivity	● Low or marginal productivity
● Quality products and services delivered on time, within budget and at competitive prices	● Poor quality products and service, unmet schedules, cost overruns and rework cause loss of good business name
● Innovation blossoms. Work methods and processes improve. New products and services are introduced. New markets are captured	● Creativity slumps. Innovation lags. Competitive threats ignored. Business loses markets to more agile competitors
● Strong current profits and excellent projections	● Poor financial picture
● The business is a good citizen of the community. Employees act legally, ethnically and in a socially and environmentally conscious manner	● Short-term interests of the business dictate environmental, social and ethical decisions. Investigations and legal actions lead to bad publicity
● Respected by the public, stockholders and competitors. Employee pride is high	● Diminished reputation and good will. Employee pride is low
● Stock appreciating. Investment capital easy to attract	● Undercapitalized, stock losing ground. Unable to attract capital
● Strong global competitor	● Uncompetitive in the global marketplace
● A bright future	● A dim future

Exercise 6 – High- and low-performance supervision

Through this exercise supervisors will begin to recognize what high- and low-performance supervision in their own areas of work might be and develop new ways for introducing high-performance practices.

Show your supervisors the table of high- and low-performance management. Invite them to look at how these characteristics might apply to their area of work. Get them to identify;

- Three examples of high-performance supervision that already exist.
- Three examples of low performance that exist and how they might turn these around to high-performance practices.
- Three new high-performance practices that they would like to introduce into their work areas.

UNDERSTANDING ORGANIZATIONAL POLITICS

Another dimension to the supervisor's role is that of becoming involved in the organization's political system. I frequently find that when I raise the issue of organizational politics with people, I get a negative response. I believe that this response is due to associating politics with control and manipulation – the abuse of the power of authority of which there is a limited resource, that is, 'the more power they have the less we have' syndrome. Although this may be true in some cases, it is a narrow view of politics in organizations. In fact, politics is an important aspect to organizational functioning.

In all organizations there are inevitably competing needs, often associated with resourcing and decision making. Developing political skills concerns influencing the right people so that your operational needs and functional responsibilities are met (for example, extra staffing, training, equipment and reward structures). The early and continued influencing of people is of prime importance from the first step on the ladder. Becoming politically aware and developing good influencing skills form an important part of a supervisor's training.

Exercise 7 – Managing in a political system

This case explores the conflicts that can result when supervisors must uphold management policies with which they disagree.

As a result of the exercise supervisors will be able to:

■ Anticipate problems new supervisors encounter in the transition from operating employee to supervisor.
■ Develop strategies for making the transition.
■ Develop solutions for typical problems supervisors experience as they accomplish work through others.

Ask your supervisors to read through the following scenario and discuss the questions with someone else. Then ask them to make a list of some answers for Deepak and consider the questions and answers in relation to *themselves.*

Scenario – He's sinking fast

Deepak, a skilled software designer, has recently been promoted to supervisor. Deepak has a reputation for delivering quality, precision work, on time. He was selected for the supervisory position because he has outstanding knowledge in computer programming and his co-workers hold him in high esteem.

After a month as a supervisor, Deepak has come to you for advice. He has had no training in management or supervision and feels he is sinking fast under his new responsibilities. He's so new to management that he is naïve about politics and procedures.

	For Deepak	For yourself
1. How can Deepak/you acquire the necessary skills in supervision before it is too late?		
2. How can Deepak/you get smart about organizational politics?		
3. What steps can Deepak/you take to build a support system?		

CONCLUSION

Gaining a good understanding of where supervisors fit into the organizational system provides the framework within which the supervisor will need to operate, now and in the future. Working with clarity is enabling and supportive, especially in political systems which often carry hidden and confusing messages. Becoming politically aware, knowing where influence needs to be executed in order to succeed, is essential to a supervisor's learning.

CHAPTER 4

MANAGING CONFLICTING LOYALTIES

KEY LEARNING POINTS

- Be able to deal with difficult issues that challenge the supervisor's authority
- Know how to manage conflicts between management decisions and staff practices

HANDLING DIFFICULT SITUATIONS

There are two particular difficulties that supervisors may encounter early in their supervisory role. The first is in maintaining good friendships already established with operational staff, but not abusing their new position by allowing favouritism. The second is in dealing with a conflict of loyalties between management and staff. There are simple strategies that supervisors can learn early in their training to avoid becoming squashed in a conflict between staff and management.

The following two exercises will help supervisors become aware of the traps that they may encounter early in their supervisory role, and learn strategies to deal effectively with difficulties that could arise.

Exercise 8 – Maintaining authority and friendships

This exercise is suitable for small groups of supervisors, as well as for individuals to think through on their own. As a result of the exercise, supervisors will be able to:

- Anticipate situations that as a new supervisor they may encounter.
- Develop strategies for dealing with the role shift.
- Develop strategies for dealing with employee requests for preferential treatment.

Get your supervisors to consider the following scenario in pairs or small groups.

Scenario – Preserving the friendship

While an office junior Barry became good friends with Talia, an employee he now supervises. Barry now thinks Talia is trying to take advantage of their friendship by asking for preferential treatment on work hours and holiday scheduling. Barry wants to preserve the friendship but he also wants to treat all his employees fairly.

The sorts of issues that Barry faces are:

- Both he and Talia must adjust to the shift in his role from co-worker and friend to supervisor.
- He needs to become comfortable with his new position of authority, and Talia must learn to respect his position as supervisor.
- If he gives preferential treatment to Talia, other staff will resent the fact that he is playing favourites.
- Teamwork and motivation will suffer.
- Workers will lose respect for both him and Talia.
- If Talia persists in trying to trade on the friendship, he will have to ask himself whether Talia is a friend at all.

How should Barry deal with the situation?

Barry needs to be clear of the outcome he is looking for. In this case it is to preserve the friendship and maintain the authority of his supervisory role.

Scenario – Managing boundaries

The following is an example of the conversation that might have occurred. It takes place at a private meeting.

Barry I need to talk to you about your holiday request.

Talia Yes, Barry, you're a good mate; I knew you would okay it. Mike and I really need this holiday.

Barry Well, I'm not so sure that it would be the right thing for me to do. If I approve this for you it would seem unfair to the rest of the team.

Talia Oh, come on, Barry, just this once wouldn't matter.

Barry feels uncomfortable; he wants to support his friend but knows that it will cause problems.

Barry I'm feeling really uncomfortable about this Talia. On the one hand I would really like to give you the holiday dates that you are asking for, on the other I feel that if I do, the team will not like it and it might even damage the good relations that both you and I have with them.

Talia looks disappointed but a considered expression crosses her face as Barry continues.

Barry I want to be fair to all of you and not give special treatment to anyone in particular. I believe that we can all work better that way.

Talia nods but remains silent.

Barry I wonder if we can look at some alternative solutions for your holiday. There are other options that fall in line with the holiday schedules which may suit you.

Talia (Smiling) Yes. Sorry Barry I was really hoping that you would agree but I can see that it would be unfair. There is another possibility ...

Barry has achieved his objective.

There were three key points that Barry needed to address in his meeting with Talia:

1. Ensuring equal treatment to all employees.
2. Looking for alternatives to Talia's apparent holiday needs.
3. Pointing out how preferential treatment could harm team spirit and Talia's relationships with her co-workers.

The trap would have been to accuse Talia of taking advantage. Such an attack would likely have led to defensiveness from Talia and possibly the loss of a friendship, as well as conflict in the team.

CONFLICT BETWEEN MANAGEMENT AND STAFF

When supervisors have not learned to deal with conflict between management and staff well, they will either shift their loyalties to one side of the fence alongside management, or to the other with their staff, or they will deny that a problem exists and go around feeling confused. None of these are satisfactory solutions. Supervisors do not want to destroy good relations with their staff, neither do they want to undermine their role as a member of the management system

Exercise 9 – Squashed in conflict between management and staff

The following exercise illustrates a typical scenario which supervisors could face. As a result of the exercise, supervisors will:

- Know how to deliver unpopular news well to staff
- Know how to carry responsibilities with both staff and management
- Learn ways of enforcing new policies with staff that conflict with current practices
- Learn how to develop solutions for typical problems that arise in their work.

Ask your supervisors to read through the scenario and answer the questions that follow. They can do this in small groups or on their own.

A skill that supervisors need to develop early on in their role is communicating information to their staff with clarity

Scenario – Delivering unpopular news

Judy has recently been promoted to a supervisory position. She has just come from a departmental staff meeting where she learned that the company has decided to take a 'hard line' on personal phone calls made from office telephones. With immediate effect employees must place all personal calls from a public pay phone.

Judy knows this will be unpopular news. In fact she disagrees with the policy, believing that the time spent finding a phone and waiting in line will cost the employer more than a brief call made from the work station. She's also concerned with the effect the policy will have on Adam, a single parent, who keeps tabs on his two sons through brief after-school phone calls.

1. What are the key points that Judy needs to consider when communicating this new policy to her employees?
2. As a member of the management team, what are Judy's responsibilities to the employer?
3. What are Judy's responsibilities to her employees?
4. How should Judy enforce the policy with Adam?

COMMUNICATING INFORMATION TO EMPLOYEES

A skill that the supervisor needs to develop early on in their role is communicating information to their staff with clarity. In my experience, lack of clarity can arise when the supervisor feels in conflict with the message they have to deliver. Keeping the communication *informative* as well as expressing these concerns will help to keep the message clear.

The following guidelines will help:

- Inform the employees (of the policy, change in practice, decisions, etc.)
- Explain the company's reason for the change/decision
- Let employees express their concerns
- Acknowledge their concerns
- Promise to inform the manager about employee concerns
- Ask for employee cooperation.

The trap here for a supervisor would be to become drawn into employee concerns rather than staying separate and maintaining an objective viewpoint.

RESPONSIBILITIES TO THE EMPLOYER

It is a responsibility of the supervisor to share their concerns with their immediate manager. In the first instance this enables them to ask for the help they need in order to support the policy in front of employees. Secondly it allows the supervisor to have the opportunity in which they themselves can air their disagreements with the company's decision.

RESPONSIBILITIES TO THE EMPLOYEES

When company decisions are made it is good practice to communicate information at the earliest opportunity to avoid employees hearing the news second hand. The supervisor needs to be clear about the business reasons behind the decision in order to communicate this as well. If they are not clear it is their responsibility to ask for this from management. It is of prime importance to listen to staff concerns on the matter. This will prevent a storm brewing and repercussions later.

Having made a promise to convey concerns to management, it is up to the supervisor to let employees know when they have done this. The principle of keeping people informed is central to the supervisor's success.

Finally, it is the responsibility of the supervirsor to ensure that new policies and practices are actioned on time and fairly, accommodating special circumstances when possible.

MANAGING UNUSUAL CIRCUMSTANCES WITHIN THE DECISION

In the scenario, Judy was concerned for Adam and his calls to his family after school. Ideally Judy would be looking to:

- Show her concern and respect for Adam's unusual circumstances.
- Look at the problem creatively, engaging in a problem-solving activity with Adam to look for other solutions and acceptable alternatives.

- Find ways of keeping within the spirit of the company's decision and to utilize the scope of her authority as a supervisor.

In unusual circumstances like this it would be appropriate to discuss the problem in a private meeting.

CONCLUSION

The supervisor stands at the first point of contact between operational staff and management. This can present difficulties, especially when some of the operational staff are also good friends. Having to maintain authority of role and sustain their friendships can be quite challenging, especially when people demand favouritism. Good inter-personal skills and a desire not to be bowled over will enable a supervisor to deal with the situation tactfully and with authority.

Dealing with conflict between management decisions and staff needs also requires tact and effective inter-personal skills. Dealing with these conflicts early will prevent much greater difficulties later. Communicating the management decision with clarity and conviction in the first place is essential.

CHAPTER 5

THE SUPERVISOR'S ROLE

KEY LEARNING POINTS

- Know and understand the different supervisory roles that supervisors will need to take on in their daily work
- Understand the expectations that people put on them to play out certain roles
- Know how to manage other people's expectations when they are not aligned with what is really needed

THE MANY HATS OF A SUPERVISOR

Supervisors will discover that their work requires them to take on a variety of roles as they interact with others. A role is a character that a person assumes in a particular situation, much like an actor plays a role in a film. With each role comes a different 'hat', a different set of skills to deal with the situation. Added to this supervisors will at times meet a conflict in the appropriate role they need to play and the 'expected role' that others put on them. In such a situation the challenge is to be able to stand their ground, to remain clear about what role will achieve the best results, and not be drawn into following other people's expectations.

Below are listed a variety of role 'hat' examples, many of which your supervisors will probably identify with.

Coaching hat	Develops plans and suggests tactics; makes assignments; encourages team members; assesses strengths and developmental needs; builds individual and team strengths by training; allows members to practice skills; gives feedback.
Team captain hat	Uses leadership and communication skills to build teams and hold them together; inspires confidence; communicates vision, mission and goals to team members; guides teams in development of objectives; helps members understand the positions they play; seeks participation in team projects: openly confronts conflicts.
Team manager hat	Encourages team members to excel; shows and builds confidence in abilities of team members; generates enthusiasm and support for team projects both within the immediate group and from the organization as a whole.
News reporter hat	Communicates information within the team; promotes the team to others.
Political analyst hat	Analyses the current politics of the business and develops strategies accordingly.
Counsellor hat	Listens to employee problems; helps employees develop solutions.
Parent hat	Supports and nurtures employees.
Negotiator hat	Is an honest broker in bringing people with different views together; negotiates for resources.
Gladiator hat	Battles to gain support or resources; fights to protect the team or project.

Hunter hat	Openly seeks new projects and sources of work for the team.
Resource allocator hat	Determines or recommends how the team's resources will be used.
Spokesperson hat	Represents the organization at professional meetings.
Detective hat	Jointly identifies problems, determines causes and develops solutions.

Exercise 10 – *Different hats for different roles*

The following exercises will help your supervisors to:

- Identify the roles that they play and the specific hats that they wear.
- Identify different hats that are related to different situations.
- Assess the roles that others expect them to play.
- Understand ways to address differences between the roles they take on and the expected roles put on them by others.

Share the list of role hats given above with your supervisors. Invite them to make a list of hats that they can identify with, which may be taken from the list or newly defined. Then get them to do this exercise and also Exercises 11 and 12.

Some typical situations are provided in column A of the following answer sheet. In column B list the roles supervisors could assume in each situation. An example is given for the first situation.

A. Situation	B. Possible roles
1. Two employees are in conflict over how to perform an assignment	● Negotiator ● Teacher
2. An employee has personal problems	
3. Another department is trying to take over facilities and equipment that are currently assigned to the supervisor's department	

A. Situation	B. Possible roles
4. The team is developing a new process, product or service	
5. The supervisor represents the organization at a civic or professional meeting	

Exercise 11 – Roles I play and roles others expect me to play

In column A of the following table list typical situations that you encounter in your work. In column B identify the role hats that you wear in those situations. In column C list the role hats that others expect you to wear in each situation.

A. Situation	B. Roles I play	C. Roles others expect me to play
1.		
2.		

A. Situation	B. Roles I play	C. Roles others expect me to play
3.		

Exercise 12 – Managing expectations

Answer questions 1–4, then identify actions that you can take to address the differences between how you view your role and how others view you.

1. What similarities are there between the roles you play and the roles others expect you to play?
2. What differences are there?
3. How do you explain the differences?
4. What can you do to address the differences?

The main reasons for difficulties arising from differences between roles played out and other people's expectations are lack of communication and clarification. The key people that the supervisor needs to clarify their roles with are their staff and their boss.

The following is an example of a situation with an employee where role expectations are not aligned. You will note how subtly this expectation finds its way into the scenario.

Scenario – Choosing the hat

Just as the supervisor is about to go home one evening a member of staff appears looking distressed. It seems that the woman is not getting on with her team and wants to move to another department because of it. She makes it quite explicit that she wants the supervisor to solve the problem for her. She is handing over the *parent hat.*

■ If the supervisor takes it and complies with the implicit *parent* role expectation, they are likely to find the same problem arising in a new team.

■ If the supervisor puts on the *team captain hat*, the one that they want to put on to deal with the problem, and ignores the *parent hat* being handed to them, they will meet resistance from the employee, which will exacerbate the problem.

The following are two options that the supervisor could take:

Difficulties arise from differences between roles played out and other people's expectations due to lack of communication and clarification

1. Clarifying the position as they see it and offering the *team captain hat* as a way of working to start with until the real problem is surfaced; for example, 'You say you would like me to move you to another department, but I'm not sure that this will solve the real problem that exists. The way I would prefer to deal with it is to spend some time with you in the morning and see if we can get to the nub of the matter, then look at the options available to us.'

2. Clarifying the problem, throwing away the *parent hat* and offering the employee the opportunity to choose a different way of working that both agree to; for example, 'You want me to move you to another department, but I wonder if there is another way of dealing with this. Have you thought of all the options?'

The immediate response of the supervisor to the employee in this situation is really important, for that is where expectations are harnessed, or challenged.

CONCLUSION

Defining roles as hats which symbolize the variety of roles that supervisors take on in their work, will help them to understand how to operate in the most advantageous way in different situations. The hats also help supervisors become aware of misaligned expectations which could otherwise lead to difficulties. Dealing with misalignment is a skill that develops with experience. The starting point is in fully understanding the part that different roles play. The more involved that supervisors are in defining their own specific hats, the more effective they will be when they take on the different roles.

CHAPTER 6

TAKING ON RESPONSIBILITIES

KEY LEARNING POINTS

- Understand the five key areas of a supervisor's responsibilities
- Know how to get the necessary knowledge, skills and experience to carry out these responsibilities well

Development into a role is not just training and coaching it is a commitment to learning

THE WHEEL OF RESPONSIBILITIES

The five connected elements shown in Figure 6.1 – purpose, tasks, procedures, people and self – all form a wheel which holds a supervisor's main responsibility areas. In keeping the wheel turning the supervisor can achieve high performance. If any one of them is dysfunctional, all the others will be affected and performance will be reduced.

We will take a look at each one of the elements in more detail.

PURPOSE

Where there is purpose there are motivated people and clear connections with the wider functional systems. Having purpose enables good alignment of departmental objectives.

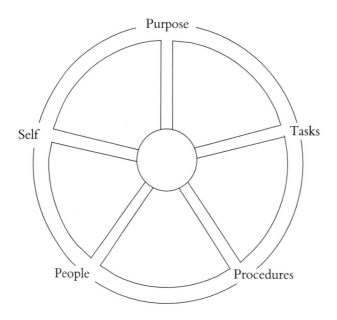

FIGURE 6.1: The wheel of responsibilities

Establishing purpose requires an understanding of the bigger picture – the mission and vision of the organization and business – and the knowledge of how personal contribution helps to achieve organizational objectives.

Clarifying purpose is key to effective leadership.

TASKS

Both technical and managerial tasks create the actions needed for achieving objectives. Clearly defined tasks enable a supervisor to assess the resources and competencies needed to carry out those tasks, as well as provide the basis for establishing procedures. Where the tasks are not clear or not well aligned with purpose, the supervisor will struggle to do either of these effectively.

With the task comes the need for clearly defined goals, objectives and benchmarking, followed by frequent reviews to assess if the task is being achieved.

PROCEDURES

Procedures are the *how* of getting tasks done efficiently.

Making plans and continual improvement methods are formal procedures that a supervisor will be responsible for.

Policy making and codes of practice are procedures that supervisors increasingly find themselves contributing to.

Leading meetings also carries a procedure, usually typical of the traditional way of holding meetings in the culture of the organization. This may be to an agenda or less formal open meetings.

PEOPLE

Managing people and harnessing their full potential is one of the key challenges facing a supervisor. The supervisor's familiarity with the technical and practical aspects of their work can easily detract from the importance of this. Helping staff develop their competencies and potential; challenging and stretching them; balancing authority with collaboration; bringing energy and enthusiasm into the department; and relating to people in a mutually beneficial way are key to achieving high performance.

SELF

There is frequently one element that is missed when developing into a new role, that is understanding ourselves. Lack of self support and self awareness can lead to emerging difficulties in our work. We have a responsibility to ourselves to make sure that we are okay. No-one else can do this for us.

You can help your supervisors pay attention to themselves by getting them to answer the following questions.

Exercise 13 – Keeping fit for high performance

- What are the key challenges facing me?
- How will this role affect my life?
- What excites me and what are my concerns?
- Where will my support be when I am struggling?
- How can I best relate to my boss?
- What will others think of me?
- What do I need to do each day to combat stress and deal with anxieties?

These questions warrant time to fully consider, You can then revisit them once in a while for a 'health check'. I like to refer to this as 'keeping fit for high performance', exercising self support in order to stay 100 per cent fit to meet the demands of the job.

Exercise 14 – The five key responsibility areas

This exercise will help raise awareness and understanding of the language and concepts used in the 'wheel' and to promote discussion about what these mean in relation to the organization. Explore and discuss the following with your supervisors:

Purpose   What is the company's mission or vision and how does its departmental objectives fit into this?

Tasks   Get your supervisors to list the known tasks that they have to carry out in their supervisory role. In general this will likely be between 6 and 12 tasks. Invite them to name some objectives linked to the tasks.

Procedures With your supervisors identify the main procedures that are in place to achieve high performance. This may be a good time to question whether these procedures can be improved.

People   Ask your supervisors to write down five skills and attributes they know they have which will help them get the best out of their staff.

Self   Get your supervisors to draw a pie chart, as shown in Figure 6.2, showing how they spend their time. This one is divided between home, work and self. On the assumption that a good balance between the three keeps a healthy mind, get them to question whether the balance is a good one for them, if not how might they change it.

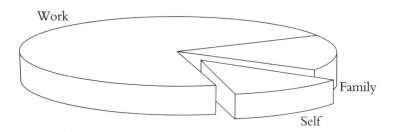

FIGURE 6.2: Pie chart showing division of time

RESPONSIBILITIES FOR THE DEVELOPMENT OF KNOWLEDGE, SKILLS AND EXPERIENCE

Supervisors have a responsibility to themselves to know how they need to develop to become proficient in their work. Development into a role is not just training and coaching, it is a commitment to learning.

Identified here are three different ways of learning, related to specific supervisory responsibilities, with comparisons between them to understand their differences.

KNOWLEDGE

Knowledge is awareness or comprehension acquired through experience, learning and study. Supervisors need the following core knowledge:

1. Solid technical knowledge about work methods and equipment.
2. Knowledge of how to manage resources, particularly human resources.
3. Organizational knowledge, particularly on policies, procedures, systemic functioning and the management system.

BUILDING KNOWLEDGE

Supervisors may ask 'what do I need to know?'. They will have their own thoughts on this. Here are some ideas of the more general points as a guide:

- A broad knowledge base of the business: customers, suppliers, competitors.
- Knowledge of the industry: who the industry leaders are, where it is heading, pace of change.
- A good knowledge of organizational functioning and a definition of some of the terminology: mission, vision, culture, values, administrative procedures, policies, rules, information and record systems.

One way of building knowledge with supervisors is to hold *study meetings* which have specific themes. For example, supervisors need to have some knowledge of personnel issues. Inviting a personnel manager to discuss recruitment or personnel policies at a study meeting would be of benefit to supervisors – and probably the personnel department as well.

SKILLS

A skill is a proficiency at performing a task and repeatedly doing the same task will develop high levels of competence and a good in-depth knowledge. Supervisors will find themselves developing new skills for their new role, such as:

- Technical skills
- Human relation skills
- Conceptual skills.

TECHNICAL SKILLS OR JOB KNOW-HOW

Technical skills refer to specific methods, techniques, tools, equipment or software, for example, operating a drill press, reading blueprints, using word processing software, dispensing prescriptions or library research. One of the biggest traps for supervisors is to continue doing operational work, rather than supervising others to do it. It can be easier and less time consuming to do the task, rather than coach others to do it. We all do this at some time or another; being aware that we do it allows choice and the possibility of change.

One of the biggest traps for supervisors is to continue doing operational work, rather than supervising others to do it

The technical skills of supervisors lie in the following areas of responsibility:

- *Production*   delivering the product or service with the available resources.
- *Quality*   stimulating quality consciousness and job pride in the workforce with a philosophy of continuous improvement.
- *Costs*   contributing to profitability and efficient use of resources by cost controlling and cost reduction.
- *Methods*   seeking easier and better ways of doing work.
- *Health and safety*   minimizing risks and hazards in the work area.

These technical areas are inter-related. Supervisors may need to build their knowledge and understanding of them in order to create a balance. For example, quality and costs often conflict illustrating the need for skilful planning. Quality can drive costs up; however over-zealous cost-cutting can result in poor quality goods reaching the marketplace.

HUMAN RELATIONS SKILLS

Human relations skills rest on an understanding of human behaviour, inter-personal communication skills and personal style. Intuition can play an important role in responding to people.

A new supervisor may not know much about managing people. One of the first changes that they will need to make is to establish their authority within their leadership role. That means building on their authority as a manager and leader without being over-controlling. Developing their own personal authority allows them to manage the balance between their role and their integrity as a human being. This is particularly important as stepping into management can lead to loss of self, oppressed by the role image, rather than integration of self into the supervisory role.

Shifting from *doing* with colleagues to empowering staff is a major change for most supervisors and takes time to adjust to. In particular, coaching skills are essential to this new role and support the responsibility that the supervisor has to the staff for training. What is important here is that the supervisor does not have to establish skills for every area of their responsibility. It is enough to have *knowledge* and *experience* of the technicalities and to develop the skills in their staff.

CONCEPTUAL SKILLS

Conceptual skills are essential for planning, problem solving, decision making, writing and public speaking. They allow managers to understand abstract or general ideas and then apply them to specific situations. The ability to see underlying patterns in seemingly unrelated events can be a great strength in management.

> Developing their own personal authority allows supervisors to manage the balance between their role and their integrity as a human being

EXPERIENCE

Experience is the breadth of our work. Constantly doing the same task does not provide good experience, even though it develops competencies. Experience is gained by being involved with a wide range of tasks, events and people. People who travel the world regularly gain the experience of viewing different cultures. Yet to become fluent and skilled in a foreign language would require that they stay in the country of origin for a period of time in order to get repeated exposure to the spoken word.

GAINING EXPERIENCE (BROADENING OUR HORIZONS)

It would be enriching for supervisors to become involved in a broad field in their work. Good experience at this level of management will pay dividends later. Ways of achieving this are:

- By encouraging contact with other supervisors both in and outside of the department.
- Getting supervisors involved in some higher management meetings.
- When they have become reasonably competent at their supervisory role, gaining work experience by sharing with other supervisors or shadowing managers.

LEARNING BY DOING

There is another dimension to experience. Much of our learning is gained through observation (vicarious learning); that is, we see someone act and imagine how it would be for us if we did that ourselves. By putting our learning into practice, that is, experience it first hand, we can integrate what we see into our own abilities to do. Imagine you are learning to ski. Without doing it, experiencing it and making mistakes, you can never claim to be able to ski. You may learn a lot by watching other people ski but it is in doing it yourself that you begin to pick up and establish the techniques.

Some people suffer stress due to a fear of failure which stops them from doing things which might fail. They never get the experience that they need to begin a learning process and to integrate what they learn. Paradoxically, this leads to failure when they set up a pretence that they are good at skills that they have never fully established.

Learning to become good supervisors will mean people taking the risk of getting it wrong. This is far better than pretending that they can do it right.

Exercise 15 – Knowledge, skills and experience matrix

Referring back to the wheel of responsibilities shown in Figure 6.1 and the questions asked in Exercise 14, get your supervisors to identify areas that interest them and areas that they need to develop in the three categories that will support them in carrying out their responsibilities well. Examples are shown in the boxes.

	Purpose	Tasks	Procedures	People	Self
Building knowledge	*Personnel legislation*		*Planning health and safety*		*Managing stress*
Developing skills			*Making a plan*	*Communication*	
Gaining experience	*Creating a vision*	*Problem solving*			*Managing difficult situations*

Having completed this matrix, supervisors can define how they will achieve their learning and assess appropriate time scales. Some learning processes will be continuous and some will be linked to this training programme.

Exercise 16 – How to gain the desired knowledge, skills and experience

Using the following table get your supervisors to list the five most important areas for development from their matrix under the relevant categories. Then identify on a scale of 1 (not skilled) to 10 (highly skilled) how good they think they are at the moment and how they would like to develop.

	Areas for development How good are you now, on a scale of 1—10	Development needs
Purpose		
Tasks		
Procedures		
People		
Self		

CONCLUSION

Many people take on new roles and responsibilities as if they have been given them because they were perceived to have the skills already. The reality is that they were probably given the job because they were seen to have the potential to do it and the capacity to learn. Supervisors need to appreciate that taking on responsibilities means learning, and that learning can be achieved in many ways. This chapter highlights three different ways to learn that supervisors can consider: knowledge, skills development and experience. A combination of all three are necessary to build good supervisory styles and to engage in their responsibilities with confidence.

PART 2

*B*UILDING THE
STRUCTURE

KEY LEARNING POINT

■ Understand a cyclical model for achieving high performance that can be used in many areas of supervision

In Part 2 a model of a cycle will be used to enable supervisors to develop skills and understanding of productive working practices. This cycle will also enable them to identify where blocks in the flow of the cycle exist when things go wrong. The cycle shown here emphasizes different phases of working practices, from responding to emerging needs, to engaging in tasks and completing them.

There will be many aspects of learning in the following chapters where supervisors can use this cycle as a model for learning and working as a high-performance supervisor. Different terminology will describe the phases in each chapter; the basic principles of the model remain the same throughout. These principles are shown in Figure P2.1.

The Cycle of Effective Working Practices

Phase 1   concerns *tuning in* to ourselves, to the workplace, to the business, to what needs there are to be met. Without a clear understanding of these, people respond only to their assumptions.

Phase 2   concerns gathering information, increasing our understanding, clarifying the need and defining purpose.

Because we are human and therefore vulnerable to human error, responding only to assumptions leads to unsatisfactory outcomes

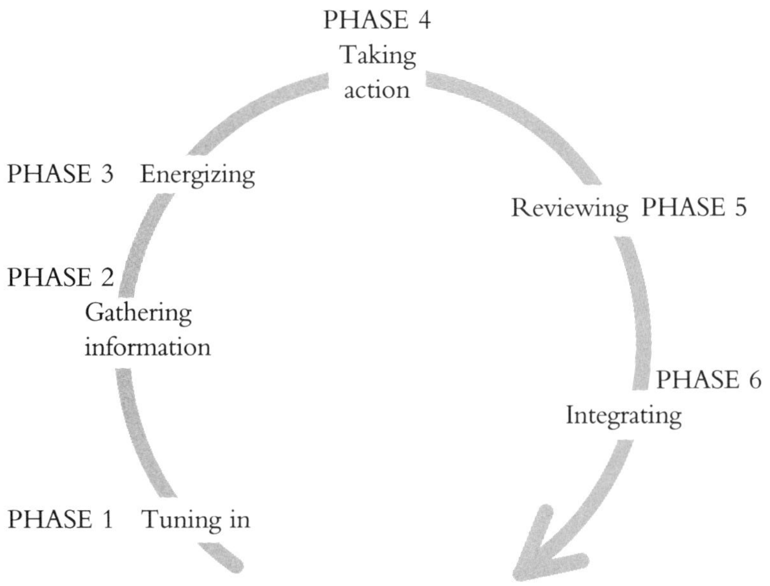

FIGURE P2.1: The cycle of effective work practices

Phase 3 can be best understood in terms of energy. That is people becoming energized, interested and motivated to get into the task. A predominant characteristic of this phase is exploring options and making choices.

Phase 4 concerns taking action, doing the task, getting into the core of the project, and includes fully engaging with a task through to full completion.

Phase 5 involves assessing, reviewing, reflecting and learning from the task and outcomes. The essence of this phase is gaining some satisfaction from what has been achieved; articulating what was good and what was not so good.

Phase 6 is a phase of integration and moving on. That is, acknowledging what has been learned and having the ability to allow that project to subside in order for a new project to emerge.

Exercise 17 – Cycle of effective working practices

Show your supervisors the cycle and talk them through the different phases. Ask them to think of an incident, task or meeting that didn't go well. With another person, see if they can identify in which phase they think they became blocked. For example:

> A meeting did not go well, important decisions had not been made because of conflict in the team. On reflection the team realized that not everyone had been given the opportunity to speak, important information that would have influenced the decision making had not been shared. Although the team appeared stuck in Phase 3 (making choices), Phase 2 (information gathering) is where they had actually been blocked.

There are many of these cycles operating at any one time. The crucial point is that in paying attention to the principles of the cycle, high performance becomes possible. When people and teams do not achieve the high performance that they seek, they can use the model to reach quick and simple understanding of where the process has become blocked.

In the following chapters we will build on this cycle. Chapter 7 develops understanding and skills for preparing and implementing plans; an important part of the operational aspect of the supervisor's role. Chapters 8–12 chart the progress of supervisors as they develop people skills and the ability to get the best out of their staff. Chapter 8 begins the process of helping supervisors manage performance through control measures. Chapter 9 develops skills for dealing with difficult situations in relation to performance management. Chapter 10 offers processes and skills for effective delegation. Chapter 11 develops processes and skills for setting goals and objectives. Chapter 12 provides useful coaching and training methods.

Chapter 13 enables supervisors to develop themselves as effective leaders. Leadership is about giving direction and clarifying purpose. It is about advising, influencing or facilitating people towards achieving a common goal. Chapter 14 focuses on getting the best out of teams and develops a different set of skills needed to achieve this. Teamwork is making the people around you feel like they are winners and champions through working towards a common goal together. This entails understanding different styles, potentials and skills which people bring into the team, and then building on them.

Chapter 15 engages with one of the most important aspects of the supervisor's role: developing and maintaining their relationship with you, their manager.

CHAPTER 7

Making and Implementing Plans

KEY LEARNING POINTS

- ■ Identify planning tasks
- ■ Understand the advantages and barriers to planning
- ■ Agree how to adjust time spent on planning different tasks
- ■ Know how to build on the key components of the planning and implementation cycle

PLANNING

Planning is the process of envisioning the future, setting goals, identifying actions to achieve goals, establishing target dates for completing the actions, and describing measures of success. Some key planning questions which supervisors can ask themselves are:

Purpose   Why is the project being done?
Vision   What outcome are you aiming to achieve?

Alignment	How does this project fit into the wider picture?
Choices	How else might the end result be attained? Where is the project being done and could it be accomplished more efficiently elsewhere?
Time	When is the project being done?
Adding Value	What technologies can we employ to increase productivity, raise quality or otherwise add value?
People	Who are the best people to work on the project?

A *plan* is a written document which serves as a roadmap that shows the way to the desired goal or destination. The plan indicates how work will be organized. Supervisors must lead in the direction mapped out in the plan. Performance is managed through standards described in the plan, such as target dates, quantities or customer satisfaction indicators.

Supervisors are planning when they:

- Create work schedules
- Develop annual budgets for their area of work
- Create a holiday schedule
- Make plans to obtain materials, tools and equipment in a timely manner
- Establish the preventive maintenance schedule for equipment
- Think about where the work unit is going in relation to the company's goals
- Develop goals and objectives for the next performance cycle
- Build a skilled and balanced work team that will be capable of meeting the work unit's future needs.

Supervisors implement plans that specify what work will be performed in their immediate work units, along with starting and completion dates. To make plans supervisors need to be able to think ahead, that is anticipate the future in order to plan for today. In the cycle, as shown in Figure 7.1,

To make plans supervisors need to be able to think ahead, that is anticipate the future, in order to plan for today

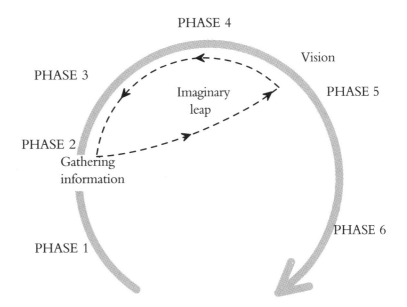

FIGURE 7.1: Creating a vision

planning comes in around Phases 2 and 3 with a visioning, imaginary leap into the future in order to establish what might be possible. Supervisors need to remain open to changing their plans, in the view that they may not have anticipated well, or that unexpected events can occur which they can not have known in advance. Plans are not cast in concrete; they can be flexible.

Exercise 18 – Planning: advantages and barriers

Get your supervisors to list their responses to the following questions:

■ What are the advantages of making plans in your area of work? (For example, it ensures that materials and supplies will be available when we need them.)

■ What are the barriers to making plans in your area of work? (For example, I'm too busy with day-to-day activities to plan.)

To help you generate the thinking of your supervisors in this exercise, listed below are lists of advantages and barriers which supervisors could generally experience. Advantages of planning include:

- It makes it possible to influence the future instead of reacting to events.
- It increases the likelihood that quality products and services will be delivered on time and within budget.
- It gives a basis from which to decide how to allocate limited resources to the most important priorities.
- It contributes to economical use of resources, for example by avoiding overtime or allowing materials to be purchased at favourable prices.
- It improves communication and coordination and helps the supervisor decide what to delegate and to whom.
- It allows the work team to measure progress through the plans, benchmarks or performance indicators.
- It heightens employee motivation to achieve goals in anticipation of agreed upon rewards and improves quality when standards described in the plan are met.
- It increases efficiency of operations and productivity.
- It helps the supervisor lead their team forward with confidence because the plan provides a destination and a roadmap.

Barriers (with challenges that might help you respond to the negatives) include:

- The supervisor and work team don't have time to plan because they are too busy with day-to-day activities. (*Planning can increase productivity, because employees have clear priorities, target dates, and the necessary resources.*)
- Circumstances change too rapidly to plan. (*Planning allows early identification of potential problems or opportunities, making it possible to develop response strategies.*)
- Those involved view planning as a waste of time. (*In the long run planning generally saves more time than it takes.*)
- Plans become obsolete almost immediately because priorities change. (*Planning creates a baseline that can be used to evaluate the relative importance of new or emerging priorities.*)

In the long run planning generally saves more time than it takes

Discuss the outcome of this exercise with your supervisors, developing a deeper understanding based on your own knowledge of the supervisor's role in your organization. In particular raise the issue that time invested in planning generally saves more time than it costs.

THE PLAN DEVELOPMENT AND IMPLEMENTATION CYCLE

Here we can use the cycle in a different way to understand all the phases required for effective planning and how implementation is supported by the written plan. The phases in this cycle, shown in Figure 7.2, relate to the basic cycle for effective working practices.

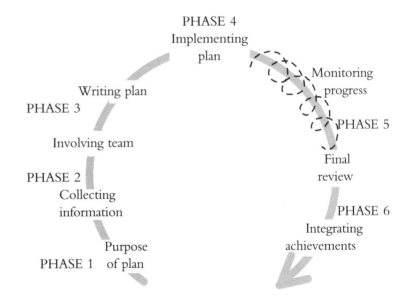

FIGURE 7.2: The plan development and implementation cycle

PHASE 1

PLANNING AHEAD
We can assume that the need for the plan is already established. It is worth conveying to your supervisors that planning without real purpose or need is a fruitless activity.

PHASES 2 AND 3

COLLECTING INFORMATION

Supervisors need to collect as much information as they can before they start pulling together their plan. Many people go rushing into action without taking time to expand their information and knowledge base about a project or task and the different ways they could approach it.

Planning requires:

- A knowledge of the history of the department i.e. last year's accomplishments
- An understanding of the current position
- Information about where management anticipates being next year
- Knowledge of any external developments that might influence the work.

INVOLVING THE TEAM

The sooner supervisors involve their team in the planning of a new project the better. There are two main reasons for this: firstly, that the team become well informed through the process; secondly, through staff involvement and contribution to the project supervisors will gain their commitment.

To involve staff, supervisors need to:

1. Describe the background
2. Seek ideas about goals and objectives.

WRITING A PLAN

I find that getting my thoughts out onto paper can help me to harness my thinking and provide a tangible structure to work with. A good question for me to ask myself is, 'If I was suddenly moved on to another project what information would my successor need in order to take this project forward?' That really focuses my thinking and writing.

The written plan will include any combination of the following: the activity; action items; responsibilities; target dates; projected timeframes; benchmarks; resources needed;

and perceived barriers. I suggest that you show your supervisors a typical written plan from your organization that they can use as a basis for developing their own.

Because of the anticipatory nature of making plans, building flexible structures is likely to be far more productive than having to adhere to a rigid and fixed plan.

Good supervisory practice would be to involve staff and their manager before and during the draft stage of writing the plan, where adjustments can be made. This involvement will undoubtedly pay off later.

PHASE 4

IMPLEMENTING THE PLAN

Planning makes it possible to influence the future rather than react to events

This is when the plan gets turned into action. Distributing the plan to employees can mark the beginning of the action phase. The trap here for the supervisor is that they start 'doing' the work rather than supervising others. Letting people know that they are accountable for agreed actions helps the supervisor avoid this trap.

MONITORING PROGRESS

A key responsibility of the supervisor is to hold regular progress reviews to keep the project on target and ensure continued efficiency. These reviews serve as a useful time to provide suggestions, encouragement and praise. Mini reviews offer opportunities to re-align the plan when results do not appear to be meeting expectations; or to make improvements that had not originally been considered.

PHASES 5 AND 6

FINAL REVIEW

The final review provides the supervisor with a good opportunity to show recognition for a job well done, through ceremonies and celebrations. Without this people feel incomplete. Fully satisfied staff are able to integrate their achievements and learning more effectively than those who are pushed into the next project too soon without due recognition. Rewards keep high performers satisfied and provide incentives and role models for others as well.

Exercise 19 – Planning tasks survey

Ask your supervisors to complete the following survey.

Look at the list in the following table and identify with a tick at the beginning of the line those tasks that you perform. After each item indicate whether the amount of time you devote to that planning task is too little, about right or too much.

Planning Tasks Survey
The amount of time I devote to this task is:

√	Planning tasks	Too little	About right	Too much
	1. Develop work schedules			
	2. Develop the budget			
	3. Develop the holiday schedule			
	4. Work with my manger to develop the department's annual goals and objectives			
	5. Work with my staff to develop their individual goals and objectives			
	6. Work with my manager to develop my goals and objectives			
	7. Develop the preventive maintenance schedule for equipment			
	8. Develop annual training plans for each employee			
	9. Make plans for acquisition of new equipment			
	10. Think about where the department is going in relation to the goals of the business			
	11. Focus resources on activities that have the highest payoff			

√	Planning tasks	Too little	About right	Too much
	12. Build a skilled, balanced work team, that will meet the department's future needs			
	13. Plan to obtain materials, tools and equipment in a timely manner			
	14. Schedule operations to utilize machinery at optimum capacity			
	15. Schedule operations to utilize people at their full potential			

Exercise 20 – Planning and implementation

Then ask your supervisors to do the same with the phases of the cycle, that is indicate how much time they spend on each activity in the planning and implementation cycle. They will likely notice a pattern of their own.

	Too little	About right	Too much
Phase 1 The purpose of the plan			
Phases 2 and 3 Gathering information Involving staff in planning Writing the plan			
Phase 4 Putting the plan into action Monitoring progress			
Phases 5 and 6 Final review			

Exercise 21 – Time for making plans

When they have completed these surveys, ask your supervisors to consider the items where they indicated too much or too little time. Invite them to explore how they might adjust the amount of time so that it is about right, suggesting they write their ideas on the following table and keep it as a reminder for the future.

Too little time

In the space below, list the steps you will take to place more emphasis on tasks to which you devote too little time.

Tasks to which I devote too little time	Actions I will take to improve the situation	Target date

Too much time

In the space below, list steps you will take to place less emphasis on tasks to which you devote too much time.

Tasks to which I devote too much time	Actions I will take to improve the situation	Target date

Good planning will
contribute to effective
performance management

CONCLUSION

Planning makes it possible to influence the future rather than react to events. The written plan provides a concrete structure on which to build effective action and make changes for the future. Paying attention to the six phases of the cycle will prevent supervisors from jumping in to write an action plan too soon, encourages them to involve their staff at an early stage in the planning and encourages good review processes.

CHAPTER 8

MANAGING PERFORMANCE

KEY LEARNING POINTS

- **Understand basic control methods**
- **Know how to communicate and implement performance standards to employees**

Managing performance is about aligning the performance of staff with set standards and controls of the organization and the department in order to achieve business objectives. Most supervisors find that they are able to manage and control resources, budgets and materials far more easily than the performance of their people. One of the reasons for this is the difficulty of selecting the targets against which to measure productivity.

PERFORMANCE MEASURES

The most common control measures are:

- *Time*   Completion schedules, benchmarks and delivery dates.
- *Quantity*   Volume of work an employee accomplishes – number of pieces produced, number of calls taken.

- *Quality* Extent to which work, products or services meet standards, specifications or customer expectations. Measures include percentage of rejects, number of complaints and customer approval ratings.
- *Cost* Amount of money spent to produce goods and services, usually in relation to budget.
- *Material* Limits on raw materials, work-in-progress materials and finished goods kept on hand. Usually stated in pounds, pieces or gallons.
- *Health and safety standards* Although this is not always recognized as a core activity, supervisors need to be aware that not keeping up with health and safety standards can result in:
  - Poor quality goods
  - Lost time through break down and accidents
  - A reduction in human resources due to absenteeism through ill health.

Good planning will support performance management. There are a number of key activities that a supervisor needs to build into their routine which will enable them to ensure good controls are maintained. The more a supervisor involves their staff in these activities the more they will spread the responsibility and increase the chances of maintaining and improving standards.

KEY CONTROL ACTIVITIES

1. Communicate performance standards to employees.
   This requires a clear understanding of performance standards. If these need reviewing or updating then now is a good opportunity.
2. Review the department's expenditures regularly to stay within budget.
3. Make sure accepted safety practices are being followed.
   By keeping in touch with health and safety professionals and involving all the staff in ensuring good practice is maintained.
4. Check output records to see if an acceptable quantity of work is being turned out on schedule.

5. See if preventive equipment maintenance is being performed regularly.
   *Keeping in touch with the maintenance department, establishing
   good relations with them, recognizing and giving them the
   importance which they deserve will likely pay off in times of
   emergency and difficulty.*
6. Make sure that materials aren't wasted.
7. Make sure that equipment isn't stolen.

Exercise 22 – Key activities for good controls

Get your supervisors to identify the key activities that they
need to pay attention to in relation to performance measures.
Then get them to indicate how often they need to do this
activity and how they might build it into their work
schedules.

Performance measures	Key activities	Scheduling in
Production		
Quality		
Costs		
Methods		
Health and safety		

When conditions change, standards and measures may need to be adjusted

When conditions change, standards and measures may need to be adjusted accordingly. For example, if a work team consistently exceeds its output quotas, the control standard could be adjusted upward. In a case where a quota appears unrealistically high, it should be revised downward.

MAINTAINING AND IMPROVING WORK STANDARDS

There are three important aspects of maintaining and improving standards:

1. Communicating set standards in terms of actions and behaviours
2. Involving staff in establishing fixed standards and setting new ones
3. Giving and encouraging regular feedback.

We can see the importance of these in relation to the cycle of effective working practices as shown in Figure 8.1.

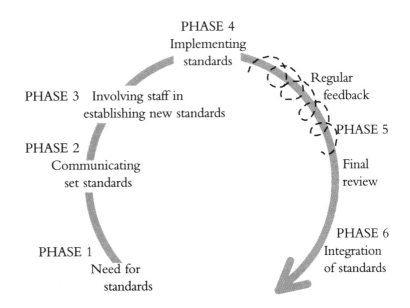

FIGURE 8.1: Cycle for maintaining and improving work standards

COMMUNICATING STANDARDS

In terms of establishing effective working practices, communicating standards is about giving information to others and clarifying it for ourselves. So it comes early in the cycle. There are three important steps to communicating information of any kind:

1. *Being clear about what it is you are going to communicate* That means really understanding the message you are giving.
2. *Communicating with clarity and crispness* Being economical with words. Many people, especially when they are nervous and not clear about what it is they are saying, say too much. The message becomes lost in a blanket of words.
3. *Making sure that people have heard the message clearly* Encouraging feedback and inviting responses for clarification. Supervisors need to be sure that the message has been heard correctly, rather than assuming this.

INVOLVING STAFF IN SETTING STANDARDS

Although managers and supervisors are responsible for ensuring standards are being met, everyone is involved in maintaining and improving them. It is in people's own best interests to be able to monitor their own performance against their goals and objectives. Encouraging involvement and initiative from staff in this will pay dividends.

It may be that the business or the industry has some generic standards to build on. For example, in the National Health Service the prime concern of nurses is patient care. There are some set basic standards that nurses have to adhere to, like ensuring that drugs are given correctly or that patient hygiene is maintained. These standards are set by a professional body such as the United Kingdom Central Council for Nursing and Midwifery. On the ward, however, nurses have the freedom to decide how they will put the set standards into action and how they can develop their own standards in a way which will add value to patient care.

In my own experience, given the power for initiative people come up with some amazing ideas, especially when

Given the power for initiative people come up with some amazing ideas

they are in an environment that will support the testing of those ideas without negative repercussions. The energy and enthusiasm that emerges from this is just lovely – a delight for any ward. The benefits to the patient – the customer – become even greater.

We can see how this works in the cycle. Phase 3 is where the energy and commitment are gained for action. The greater the commitment, the more effective the action.

BLOCKED ENERGY

Commitment is gained through purpose, clear communication and involvement. Without involvement, implementation is not carried through with the same energy; the energy is depressed and a vicious cycle set up.

The following cycle, in Figure 8.2, illustrates this with the example of setting standards for patient care. The consequences of not involving staff in agreeing how they can meet standards and introduce new ones results in depressed energy, which in turn results in poor standards on the wards.

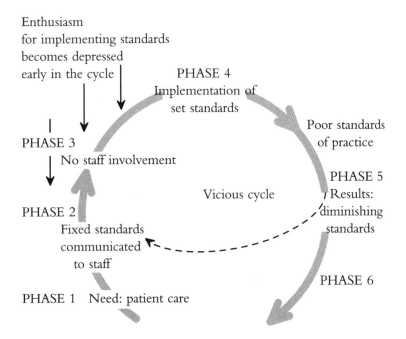

FIGURE 8.2: Blocked energy in the cycle

Notice that the problem starts before implementation, but becomes apparent in the implementation phase (Phase 4). When people's hearts aren't in it, standards will slip.

To management, the problem appears linked to applying standards on the wards, that is in Phase 4. In fact it is more likely to be linked to Phases 2 and 3, much earlier in the cycle. Without this knowledge management can only respond to what they see. Believing that they need to re-emphasize the standards that nurses and staff have to adhere to, they fall into a vicious repetitive cycle which fails to reach satisfactory completion and improved standards.

GIVING AND ENCOURAGING REGULAR FEEDBACK

Now we move to the latter end of the cycle, Phase 5, where the standards are in action and there is a need for regular feedback to ensure efficiency and make adjustments where necessary. This feedback involves a two-way process:

1. Giving spontaneous recognition of good practice
2. Inviting facts and views from outcomes of actions taken, and their effectiveness in relation to the purpose.

Regular two-way feedback supports continual improvement.

Giving staff the responsibility of maintaining and improving standards will support high-performance super-vision.

Exercise 23 – Setting standards

Get your supervisors to identify some of the standards that are already established in their area of work. Get them to explain how these are put into practice. Invite them to consider what other standards of practice and behaviour could be developed that might help improve performance. Ask them what people would be doing differently if these standards were put into practice. Then ask them to assess their communication skills on a scale of 1 (not good) to 10 (very good) using the table opposite.

	How good are you on a scale of 1—10?	What action can you take to develop your skills further?
Making sure you understand the message you are conveying to others	1 2 3 4 5 6 7 8 9 10	
Delivering a message clearly and crisply	1 2 3 4 5 6 7 8 9 10	
Checking that people have received the message correctly	1 2 3 4 5 6 7 8 9 10	
Clarifying, for the understanding of others	1 2 3 4 5 6 7 8 9 10	

CONCLUSION

The first step into managing performance is being clear about where and how measurements can be made. Second, supervisors need to have the skills to communicate standards to their staff, involving them where possible in setting specific standards in relation to the work area. However it is worth mentioning that too many rules and regulations can have a negative effect, as can rules that are too rigid and inflexible. Continuous review of standards will ensure that flexible, effective methods are sustained.

CHAPTER 9

DEALING WITH DIFFICULT SITUATIONS

KEY LEARNING POINT

■ Skills for dealing with difficult situations

DEALING WITH DIFFICULT SITUATIONS

It is all very well explaining to supervisors how to get performance management right. But what do they do when things go wrong? Operational issues are usually the easiest to put right. Dealing with behavioural issues is more difficult, especially when friends are involved.

Difficult situations often arise through people's behaviour or attitudes, and more often than not the problem belongs to the person who cannot deal with the behaviour or attitude. The answer is to tease out the threads that are knotted together in the situation rather than assume that a particular person is 'the problem'.

Exercise 24 – Dealing with difficult situations

Get your supervisors to read the following scenario then answer the questions below. Your supervisors could work in pairs and role play how they might approach the situation.

Scenario – Quality is below standard

Recently Diane was selected to head the branch where she had worked for two years. Over that period Diane socialized frequently with her co-worker, Alison. Diane values her friendship with Alison. Three times since being promoted, Diane has met with Alison to discuss a work project that is not going according to plan. Each time Alison has thrown a tantrum and has accused Diane of picking on her.

Today Diane is meeting with Alison to discuss the project, which is two weeks behind schedule.

1. What issues are involved?
2. How should Diane open the meeting?
3. What topics should Diane discuss with Alison?
4. How should Diane respond to Alison's tantrums?
5. How should Diane close the meeting?

Let's look at how one possible scenario might have been played out.

Diane has set up a meeting in her office for 11.30 a.m. Having given some thought to the issues involved she realizes that her role shift is causing both her and Alison some difficulty. Diane realizes that she is not good at delegating to Alison or setting standards for the work that she does. Also of importance is their friendship. On the other hand, she has noticed that Alison does not treat her co-workers with respect, herself neither come to that. She certainly has not been good at meeting project deadlines recently.

Alison arrives at 11.30 on the dot which Diane thinks is a good sign. Alison is wearing a forced smile and suggests that they discuss things over coffee. Cautious about turning this important meeting into a social event, Diane declines. She motions Alison to take a seat and immediately takes the initiative and shows her authority.

Diane   What I want to discuss with you, Alison, is this project, which is still behind schedule.

Alison starts turning red, her smile dropping into her lap.

Diane   I want to find a way of helping you but you seem to get so cross every time I raise it. I'm not picking on you, I really want to help.

Alison   I do feel got at. No-one ever seems to listen to my side of the argument.

Diane   Well, looking back at the records you did agree to complete this by the end of last month. Maybe you would like to tell me yourself what the problem is.

Alison retorted through a half suppressed tantrum.

Alison   Yes, I did agree to complete this by the end of the month, then I got dragged in to finish off Bill's work and then Lucy went off sick. I'm not a robot you know!

Diane felt her blood rising; she kept saying to herself 'stay calm, stay calm – focus on the purpose of this, not the feelings'.

Diane   I realize that you have had extra pressures. The way I would prefer us to work is that we renegotiate your schedule when things get in the way. Without knowing the difficulties you are having I assume that you are okay. When you don't finish your project on time it affects my deadlines and the work of the whole department. (With a final release of energy) then I have to answer to my boss!

Diane felt an inner sigh, she could see she had been heard at last by Alison. In the past Alison's tantrums had stopped this from happening.

Alison   So what now?

> **Diane**   What help would you need to get the project finished by the end of this week?
>
> The conversation continued to a useful end with a revised schedule, extra resources for Alison and a saved friendship. In her heart Diane knew that Alison was quite capable of delivering. Diane was pleased with the meeting and that she had managed to sustain her authority.

Diane made some enquiries before the meeting as to how she might handle the situation she was faced with. Her familiar approach had not worked. She discovered the following tips.

BEFORE THE MEETING

- Define the 'problem' behaviour
- Be clear about what issues are involved
- Decide what needs to be discussed at the meeting.

AT THE MEETING

- Seek understanding of the cause or origin of the problem 'behaviour'
- Remain calm
- Explore ways of seeing the events surrounding the problem in a different light
- Acknowledge the feelings exhibited by the employee
- Reflect back what is being said, paying particular attention to words of an extreme nature like *always* or *never*
- Seek alternative ways of dealing with the circumstances surrounding the problem
- Be clear about where responsibilities exist.

CLOSING THE MEETING

- Check that you have a common understanding of what you have jointly agreed
- Remind the employee of the consequences of not living up to the agreement
- Express confidence in their ability to meet the agreement, reminding them of your availability if difficulties arise again.

AFTER THE MEETING

■ Give feedback and encouragement on progress.

CONCLUSION

If we work with the attitude that people are not the problem, that it is a set of circumstances and behaviours that have culminated in a problem, then we step out of a paradigm of *blame* into a paradigm of resolution. We can deal with the circumstances and adjust behaviour once we have separated them. It is when they become intertwined and treated as one single problem that supervisors will find themselves trying to resolve an impossible, tangled knot.

CHAPTER 10

DELEGATING

KEY LEARNING POINTS

■ Know how to get the best out of staff
■ Be able to delegate to get the desired results

Managing people is about getting results. It is about getting people to do things, preferably through their interest in and commitment to the work, rather than through authoritative command.

In the past the emphasis for getting results has been on technical competence and motivating people to do the job. Directive and controlling management (and keeping people in order) can achieve the desired outcomes. Today, however, our deepening understanding of people is leading to more collaborative approaches to getting results through the efforts of employees. Tapping into people's energy and interest in their work, getting staff involved in decision making and problem solving, and operating with a philosophy for learning enables supervisors to bring out the best in their staff.

As your supervisors' manager, your role in this is not only to support their development and learning, but also to model ways of working that you would like to see them emulate.

DELEGATING

Delegation is assigning authority and responsibility to others so that they can do what is necessary to complete the job. When supervisors delegate, they accomplish the results for which they are accountable by empowering others.

When supervisors delegate, they accomplish the results for which they are accountable by empowering others

Authority gives a supervisor the right to make decisions, carry out actions and direct others. When a supervisor delegates authority, the degree of authority granted can range from none to full authority:

- *Full authority*   Allows the employee to decide and act without consulting a superior.
- *Limited authority*   Allows the employee to make decisions and take action, reporting to their superior when they feel the need or through prior agreement.
- *No authority*   This is quite different. The employee recommends action, seeking advice and approval before taking action, or can only take action on instruction from their superior.

It is unrealistic and unfair to assign responsibility to employees without giving them sufficient authority to accomplish their task. Authority and responsibility must coincide.

Supervisors can delegate authority, but they are still accountable to upper management and to the business for both the successes of and mistakes made by employees. That is a responsibility of their job; as it is the responsibility of every manager in the organization. Delegating authority is not giving away the responsibility that the supervisor holds. Supervisors are expected to have good judgement on the authority that they assign to employees; as you, their manager, used your judgement in assigning authority to them when they were recruited.

There are four important factors that supervisors need to pay attention to when delegating:

1. That they apply a philosophy for learning; so people do not feel the pressure to get it right first time and the supervisors support the learning process.

Supervisors can delegate
authority, but they are still
accountable to upper
management and to the
business for both the
successes of and mistakes
made by employees

2. That the appropriate level of authority is given and that the supervisors carry their own responsibility for the delegated work.
3. That they let go of the authority they have delegated; giving authority on the one hand and then taking it back on the other conveys mixed messages and will diminish the level of trust that employees have in their supervisors.
4. That they delegate to add value to the work of the department, not as a dumping ground for all the jobs that they do not like doing.

Exercise 25 – The benefits of and barriers to delegating

Get your supervisors to explore the benefits of and barriers to delegating in their field of work. Encourage them to be specific in relation to jobs, people and how delegation adds value to achieving the department's objectives.

The sort of benefits that they might come up with are that delegation:

- Increases productivity
- Strengthens the work of the team by building back-up capabilities for peak load times, holidays or emergencies
- Provides variety in assignments, broadens people's work experience which increases job satisfaction and fights boredom
- Allows both employees and management to see the employees' capabilities
- Provides opportunities to learn
- Creates challenge and engenders motivation
- Can induce self esteem and pride
- Can lead to better decision making
- Can produce results faster.

Delegation is frequently
misperceived as simply
passing on tasks to
employees

Barriers to delegation (with challenging comments) might be:

- Time taken to teach employees (*Training and coaching employees to do recurring jobs saves the supervisor time in the long run.*)
- Reluctance to give up preferred activities (*The importance of the supervisor's role is that they achieve results through others.*)
- Deadlines too close (*Being in this predicament suggests that planning is insufficient or not being adhered to, or that employees need skill training.*)
- Lack of confidence in others (*To discover and build upon employees' skills requires that the supervisor delegate more, not less.*)
- Fear of losing control (*Control is about letting go of some authority with confidence, not holding on to it.*)
- Concern that an employee may be able to do the job better than the supervisor has in the past (*When employees shine it reflects on the supervisor and their capacity to develop people to a high standard.*)
- Concern that they will be resented by employees (*Delegation can build employee motivation and confidence. Not delegating can cause resentment and undermine people's confidence.*)

The phases in the delegation cycle are shown in Figure 10.1.

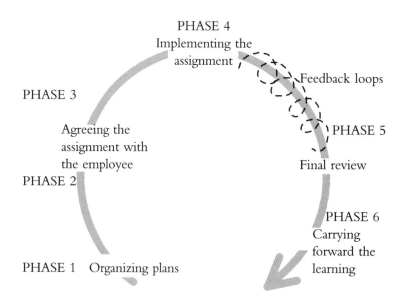

FIGURE 10.1: The delegation cycle

PHASE 1

When it comes to the act of delegating assignments to employees we can assume that the supervisor has already established plans for their area of work and considered how tasks will be achieved. They then need to divide responsibilities among employees and decide how much authority to transfer. In doing this the supervisor needs to be aware of employees':

- Capabilities
- Interests
- Experience
- Current work priorities.

The supervisor may need to adjust the work load to free an employee for an assignment. The *delegation planning sheet* provided will help the supervisor to clarify their decisions.

Delegation Planning Sheet

The assignment
1. Describe the assignment you want to delegate.
2. List all the tasks involved in meeting the assignment.
3. What will the end result look like?
4. What is the desired completion date?
5. What is the budget?
6. Describe any known constraints.
7. What alternative methods do you have for accomplishing this task?

The employee
8. Who do you wish to delegate the assignment to?
9. On a scale from 1 (lowest) to 5 (highest) rate the employee's readiness to take on the assignment.
10. Describe in detail the level of authority that you intend to invest in the employee, e.g. limited authority – require consultation on decisions befor' action is taken.
11. Wha⎱ informs you that the employee can perform the job to the standard that you expect?
12. How does this assignment relate to other priorities that you have given the employee?

Exercise 26 – Using the delegation planning sheet

Get your supervisors to think of an assignment in their work area that they would like to delegate. Decide who they could delegate it to and describe how this could add value to the work of the department. It might be useful to refer to written plans that they have already established.

Then complete a delegation planning sheet.

PHASES 2 AND 3

Agreeing the project with the employee involves circling around Phases 2 and 3 of the cycle. To do this the skills required of a supervisor are:

- *Clear, crisp language* To communicate clearly the background of the assignment and why the employee was selected for the job.
- *The ability to engage well and to listen* To discuss the advantages for the employee and invite the employee's response to the initiative.
- *Clarification skills* To clarify the desired outcome and encourage questioning.
- *Skills for working with staff collaboratively* Discuss what has to be done and how.
- *Negotiation skills and the ability to work flexibly* To agree the scope of the assignment, i.e. work methods, dates, place, budgets, performance measures.
- *Holding authority* To discuss and agree the level of authority to be attributed to the assignment.

By the end of Phase 3 the employee should be enthusiastic about their assignment, clear about what is expected of them and committed to the level of authority that they are taking on.

Exercise 27 — Dealing with difficult situations in the delegation process

Get your supervisors to discuss how they would deal with the following situation, making a list of the issues that they think may exist.

Scenario — The ambivalent employee

You are in the middle of Phases 2 and 3 and your employee is showing no signs of enthusiasm for the assignment. You feel that they really aren't interested and, although agreeable to what you are saying, they are not really engaged with you. You feel like you are in a one-way conversation. You are concerned about their commitment.

The supervisor needs to pay attention to the following issues when delegation becomes difficult:

1. They should check out any assumptions they are making about the employee's behaviour, e.g. silence does not mean 'not interested'.
2. They should check their own style. There may be something said by the employee that was really important that they didn't fully hear.
3. They should find out if the employee feels confident about doing the work and if they are not how they can support them. They can boost the confidence of the employee by giving specific examples of their past performance which were very good.
4. If the employee has a legitimate concern they may need to modify the assignment, or give the job to someone else.
5. If the worker remains uncooperative they may need to recognize their own limitations and consult their manager to evaluate alternatives.

PHASE 4

Having delegated the assignment the supervisor's responsibility is to support the employee by providing them with the time and resources to do the job.

Empowerment comes about in two ways:

1. By letting other employees know of the assignment and seeking their cooperation.
2. By supporting the employee in their ability to complete the assignment, through tracking progress and creating a balance between useful feedback and keeping a distance to let the responsible employee do the job.

Exercise 28 – Uncooperative employees

There may be occasions when supervisors have to exert their authority when employees bypass the authority given to someone on a delegated assignment. Ask your supervisors how they might deal with this.

PHASES 5 AND 6

The final two phases of the delegation cycle involve reviewing the completed assignment and carrying forward the learning. This is an opportunity to enable reflective learning for the employee and to give recognition for good work achieved. This is also a useful time to recognize how the assignment has contributed to the wider achievements of the department.

Exercise 29 – Skills assessment

Get your supervisors to assess themselves on the following skills and agree what they need to do to develop the skills areas in which their assessment is low.

Another way of making this assessment is to invite your supervisors to work in pairs or groups of three, where peers do the assessment. Referring back to Exercise 26, each supervisor picks up from their delegation planning sheet and sets up a role play for Phases 2 and 3. This is a more risky exercise to do but, as with all learning, offers a good opportunity to practice skills development in an environment that is safer than a real life situation.

Supervisors take it in turns to play the employee and practice their skills as a supervisor.

To build on this supervisors could role play dealing with ambivalent employees as shown in Exercise 27.

These exercises also offer a good opportunity to practice the skills of constructive feedback in a peer group setting.

Delegation skills	Not very good	About average	Excellent
Communicates information in clear, crisp language			
Engages with the employee			
Listens to and really hears what is being said			
Clarifies the desired outcome			
Seeks clarification from the employee about their thoughts and concerns			
Encourages questioning			
Works collaboratively			
Shows a willingness and ability to negotiate			
Holds their authority			
Offers support			

CONCLUSION

Delegation is frequently misperceived as simply passing on tasks to employees. As we have shown here the process of delegation takes on a much more fundamental role in the organization's activities, especially in performance management. Developing the skills for effective delegation will support the supervisor, releasing them from operational activities and offering the opportunity to develop the skills of good management practice.

CHAPTER 11

SETTING GOALS AND OBJECTIVES

KEY LEARNING POINTS

■ **Know how to set goals**
■ **Know how to write SMART objectives**
■ **Understand the process for setting goals with staff**

Goals are desired end results and are related to key result areas. Goal statements describe what results the business or department aims to achieve within a given time limit, for example, we aim to train all our staff to use the Internet competently by the end of July this year.

Key result areas are subject areas where high performance is essential to fulfilling the company's vision. Potential key result areas include:

- Productivity
- Customer service
- Process improvements
- Health and safety
- Outputs
- Cost reduction

- Quality
- Innovation
- Training
- Error reduction
- Time conservation
- Environmental responsibility.

Each business and department will have their own specific key result areas.

Objectives are statements that describe actions to achieve a goal. It takes a series of actions to achieve a goal. The use of an acronym SMART will help you to remember essential criteria for setting objectives:

- **S**pecific   Written in a clear language that describes what will be done and by whom.
- **M**easurable   Objectives should contain a standard of performance by which success can be measured. You should know clearly when the objective is achieved.
- **A**chievable   Creating too much of a challenge, e.g. unrealistic completion dates, will lead to people feeling deflated and unwilling to commit to future goals; too easy a goal and people will become complacent and bored.
- **R**esources   Resources such as staff, equipment, space and funds must be available or obtainable.
- **T**ime-limited   Objectives must include a clearly identified time element. Without this objectives can end up as unfulfilled wishes.

Well crafted objectives meet the SMART criteria. The following are some examples of good objective statements:

- We will train all staff to use the Internet by the end of July. Trainers will be drawn from the IT department.
- By the end of September this year all employees will have PCs on their desks.
- Each sales person will be expected to introduce three new customers a month over the next six months.
- There will be 10 new trees, of different species, planted around the park this autumn.

Exercise 30 – Identifying key result areas

Get your supervisors to identify the key result areas in their field of responsibility. Then ask them how these key result areas contribute to the business.

Ask them what would be a reasonable goal that they might

expect themselves to achieve in relation to this key result area. Then ask them to write down some SMART objectives for achieving this goal.

SETTING GOALS AND OBJECTIVES WITH EMPLOYEES

In many industries in the past employees have relied on management to set their goals for them and have often been heavily reprimanded for not achieving them or rewarded through bonuses when they have. With new ways of working and new management styles, managing the performance of employees through setting goals and objectives is becoming far more collaborative. Collaborative goal setting requires skills: good inter-personal skills, an influential style and an ability to empower and motivate employees. Most people are not naturally good at this, these skills take practice and a clear understanding of what makes people tick. Putting skills into practice at work demands an environment that supports learning. Figure 11.1 shows the phases in the collaborative goal setting cycle.

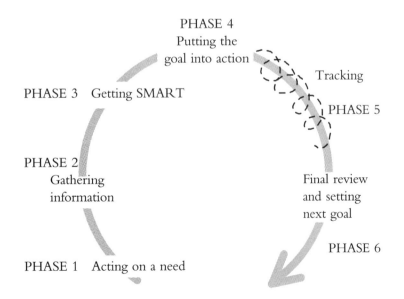

FIGURE 11.1: Collaborative goal setting cycle

The following scenario describes how a national dairy Company, MilkO, put the skills for collaborative goal setting into practice in their local depots.

Scenario — The declining sales of MilkO

With declining milk sales on door step deliveries, MilkO decided that they needed to increase the sales and delivery of other products on the milk rounds. These products were mainly eggs, cheese, butter, cream, yoghurts, chicken and bacon. Traditionally these products were offered as a service. MilkO had never attempted to really push sales of these products and decided to encourage the milk rounds staff to try and sell more when collecting money on Fridays and Saturdays. This would be achieved through the depot managers and supervisors goal setting with the rounds staff. MilkO decided that they would probably achieve more if they used a collaborative approach to this. All depot managers and supervisors were trained to use the collaborative goal setting model.

Phase 1 – The need
The need was apparent -- without a radical change the business would go under. MilkO established targets with each depot based on key result areas. Geographical position and the type of people in the locality were factors in this decision-making process. The depot managers had to meet these targets through the rounds people.

Phase 2 – The history and current sales records
Each rounds person was assessed in relation to their round. Good sales records had always been kept on a weekly basis so measurements could be made against the previous year's records, week number by week number. The supervisors, who were each responsible for a number of rounds, agreed their targets with the depot manager and received training

to goal set with the rounds people using a collaborative approach. Rewards for increased sales were based on the current reward structure.

Phase 3 – Getting SMART

The supervisors met with each rounds person, taking them through a goal setting process. The purpose of this was to agree product sales goals for the rounds and to motivate rounds people to push their sales up. The process for this was:

- Allowing time to get to know the rounds person; good listening skills and appropriate sharing of themselves helped this process.
  Getting to know a person in this way can provide useful information as to what motivates them.
- Giving clear information about the decline in the industry, the impact on the company and the effects on the depot with target information and the supervisors' own goals.
- Focusing in on what might be possible in terms of setting goals for that particular round. Important aspects of this were assessing the confidence of the rounds person in their ability to sell and recognizing the local competition that might create challenges for the rounds person.
- Establishing 'what's in it for me', that is what the incentive would be for the rounds person to put extra time and effort into increasing sales. The reward structure did not offer good incentives, so supervisors had to seek out other ideas for motivating staff. Typical ideas that they came up with were:
  - Offering weekly depot prizes
  - Inviting the rounds people to suggest ideas
  - Sponsoring charities that rounds people were involved in locally, e.g. for each pack of eggs sold the depot would pay 5p towards the purchase of talking books for the visually impaired
  - Visiting other rounds to learn how to sell from each other

Of real importance is that employees own the goals that they commit themselves to achieving

- Loser of the week cleaning the winner's milk float
- Putting sales graphs of each round in the staff room
- Supporting each other in an extra day off for exceptional sales
- Setting up competition between depots.

■ Recording the agreed goal and objectives established using the SMART model. Supervisors also established what level of support each rounds person would need to increase their sales.

Phase 4 – Tracking

The next step for the supervisors was to keep in touch with their rounds people as they actioned their objectives. At times they would even go out on the round with them. The main purpose for this was to keep track of the progress being made and give feedback, support and recognition. Sometimes they simply needed to leave the rounds people to get on with it.

Phases 5 and 6 – Review and setting next goals

Supervisors set up regular meetings with their rounds people for reviewing achievements and goal setting for the coming period. Supervisors would at times bring all the rounds people together to celebrate their achievements. This phase also included reflection on what was not achieved and gave an opportunity to discover where the problem was that prevented goals being reached. This included recognizing over-optimistic behaviour from rounds people, lack of interest, not enough support and so on. Reflection and review offered a real opportunity to learn and improve.

MilkO's dairy product sales increased.

Exercise 31 – Managing staff performance

Reflecting back on Exercise 30, where supervisors identified their own goals and objectives in relation to their key result areas, get them to answer the following:

1. With each of your staff identify their key result areas that you could set goals against.
2. What measurements can you use to set goals and objectives for your staff against?
3. Name five skills that you need in order to work collaboratively with your staff in agreeing and achieving their goals.
4. Which of these skills do you need to improve?
5. How can you practice your skills?
6. Generate five ideas that you could use as incentives.
7. What support might your staff need to achieve their goals?
8. What difficulties do you imagine you might encounter with your staff in using a collaborative process?

CONCLUSION

Managing the performance of staff means being involved with them and the way they work. Using a collaborative approach to goal setting and involving them in using the SMART model for setting objectives will achieve this. Of real importance is that employees own the goals that they commit themselves to achieving. Ownership also means that there is something in it for them, this may simply be that they openly receive recognition or improve their credibility. The skilful supervisor needs to be creative about incentives and not make assumptions about what motivates different people. Supporting each other in dealing with the difficulties that they encounter will help supervisors develop the skills for achieving high performance in their staff.

CHAPTER 12

Training and Coaching Staff

KEY LEARNING POINTS

- Understand the difference between training and coaching
- Be able to train staff through an interactive process
- Know how to coach staff to improve their performance

MANAGING PERFORMANCE THROUGH COACHING AND TRAINING

One of the supervisor's tasks will be to train and coach their staff in new skills and to improve their performance. They might already have been confronted by this need through both delegation and goal setting. Different professions have a different view as to the contrast between coaching and training. To help supervisors support the learning of their staff they are differentiated here as follows.

Training is the process of passing on skills and techniques. The trainer is expected to fully understand the skills they are passing on. Their role is mainly one of instruction. *Coaching* is on-going support for establishing and improving peoples' performance. In a sense coaching is about releasing people's potential. The coach does not necessarily have to be practised

For the best learning to occur the supervisor will need to engage with the employee in the learning in the skill that the trainee is learning, for example athletes are often coached by people who are knowledgeable about the sport but have not excelled at it. It is useful for supervisors to be able to coach because:

1. It means that they don't have to be skilled in all the areas that they are responsible for in order to coach others to do the work.
2. It means that they have a method for supporting the continual improvement of people's performance.

Characteristic of good practice for both of these learning methods is that they embrace two-way interaction; effective learning is far from passive. For the best learning to occur the supervisor will need to engage with the employee in the learning. The following cycle (shown in Figure 12.1) and definitions describe how this can happen.

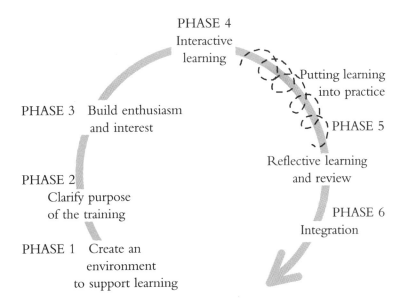

PHASE 4
Interactive
learning

Putting learning
into practice

PHASE 3   Build enthusiasm
and interest

PHASE 5

Reflective learning
and review

PHASE 2
Clarify purpose
of the training

PHASE 6
Integration

PHASE 1   Create an
environment
to support learning

FIGURE 12.1: The interactive cycle for learning

The following descriptions of each phase provide supervisors with pointers to help them engage with trainees and the learning process.

PHASE 1

Create an environment that will support learning and development. If people feel unsafe, or fear reprimand if they do not get it right, they will not take the risk of putting their skills into practice and of course will not learn or integrate learning.

- Support means being able to: ask for help; make mistakes; ask for clarification; decide that there are some jobs some people will never do well; have peers who can help; take time out to think.
- Cultures which carry blame, cynicism and criticism do not provide support for learning.

PHASE 2

Be clear about the purpose of the training or coaching to the trainee. It is helpful for them to see how their skills and development fit into the wider picture.

Describe the end result or show samples of the finished product.

PHASE 3

Check that the trainee is interested in learning. A good indicator is the level of energy and enthusiasm exhibited by the trainee. People will only learn if there is need or interest. Disinterested people do not learn well.

If supervisors sense that a trainee is not interested, now is the time to inspire them or consider another area for their development.

PHASE 4

Invite trainees to influence the way you work with them to help them learn. There are four well known methods:

- *Conceptually* Understanding the theory or idea behind the skill.
- *Vicariously* To be shown or learn through the modelling of others.
- *Experientially* To put skills into practice or to learn through discovery.

■ *Reflectively*   To review and reflect on actions that have been taken.

Usually a combination of methods is best; especially including experiential learning. I described in Chapter 6 how it is impossible to claim one can ski through vicarious or conceptual learning without putting instructions into practice. 'Show and have-a-go' is a useful approach to simple skills development.

Different people learn in different ways. It is easy and convenient for us to assume that people learn the same way that we do ourselves; it is a serious misjudgement when trainers do this.

To assume that people learn the same way that we do ourselves is a serious misjudgement

Keep in mind that although someone may understand how to do a skill they may not have the technical aptitude or physical strength to do the work, for example changing a tyre on a car.

Pay attention to levels of energy throughout the learning process. Body language is a good indicator of this. If energy drops then there is a likelihood that learning capacity is declining. It is better to stop training or coaching and engage in discussion or resume other tasks for a while.

PHASES 5 AND 6

Review progress and support integration. Reviewing is about giving and receiving feedback for both supervisor and trainee. The fact that a trainee may not be learning well could say more about the supervisor's style than the trainee's interest and ability to learn. It is the ultimate responsibility of the supervisor to ensure that good learning is taking place, even if it means that they adjust their style to meet the needs of the trainee.

Check on progress frequently until the employee exhibits full competency of the skill. Then check occasionally to let the employee know that they are important and appreciated while integration is taking place. If bad habits start forming redirect the behaviour.

TRAINING

The following is an exercise that will help your supervisors develop skills in training, and put the interactive cycle into practice in a role play. The exercise is fun to do and will help supervisors practise skills in a safe environment.

Exercise 32 – Special Occasions gift wrap

Get your supervisors to practise their skills for giving and following instructions, by doing the following role play. They can work in groups of three, one person to take on the role of a supervisor, one person to take on the role of the employee and the third person to observe.

Supervisor

You supervise a department at Special Occasions that is responsible for gift wrapping and decorating customers' purchases. The business prides itself on the extra touches it gives to its products such as special methods for wrapping and adding handmade multi-looped bows.

An employee with no prior experience in wrapping and bow making has just reported to work. You must explain the assignment and teach the individual how to wrap and decorate parcels to the quality standards expected.

You decide to start with a simple shape to wrap, like a book. You require brown paper or gift wrap, gift ribbon, scissors and glue. You will need to be clear beforehand what specifically you want your trainee to learn, that is, the detailed and unique aspects of wrapping techniques – the essential skills to transfer.

During the skill practice be aware of the following:

1. What difficulties you are having in transferring the skill.
2. What techniques are working best.
3. What you could do differently.
4. How well you are able to follow the interactive cycle.

Employee

You have just reported for your first day in the gift wrapping department of Special Occasions and you are meeting the supervisor who will explain your responsibilities. Your job is to wrap and decorate customers' purchases. You have no prior experience in this work.

During the exercise follow the instructions given by your supervisor to the letter. If the supervisor asks 'Do you understand?', nod and say 'Yes'.

During the skill practice be aware of the following:

1. What difficulties you are having in picking up the skill and why.
2. What the supervisor is doing that is helpful.
3. What else the supervisor could do to help you master the skill more quickly.
4. What you could have done to help the supervisor teach you the skill.

Observer

As you observe the skill practice watch for the following:

1. How interactive is the supervisor with the trainee throughout the exercise?
2. What communication techniques does the supervisor use to help the employee learn the skill?
3. What behaviours does the supervisor use that make it more difficult for the employee to learn the skill?
4. What does the employee do to help the learning process?
5. What does the employee do that inhibits the process?

Following the exercise, review together referring back to the points raised under each role, then do the exercise again changing roles.

Some difficulties that the supervisor might instigate:

- Use complicated language
- Make the task sound more difficult than it is
- Display a lack of interest or confidence in the employee
- Leave out steps in the process
- Communicate in a patronizing way, e.g. 'Have I made myself clear?'
- Show impatience or frustration
- Fail to get the employee to practise the process.

What the employee might do to inhibit the learning:

- Appear disinterested
- Be overconfident

- Resent being asked to practise
- Not listen and watch
- Not ask questions
- Be too creative
- Not ask for clarification.

Sometimes the more a person knows about a task the more difficult it is to teach another person how to perform it. This is usually because the skill for doing the task is so well integrated in the mind that the trainer forgets to mention essential steps. A way around this is to list all the mini-steps and special techniques beforehand and invite a co-worker to review the list.

COACHING

The most commonly understood coaching practice is within the world of sport. The purpose of the coach is to develop the skills of the sportsperson to a high standard of performance, in an encouraging and challenging way. Coaching is not telling people what to do. One of the role hats of a supervisor is that of a coach.

In the coaching process the employee can take on a more active role, stating what it is they want help with; what skills they wish to improve; maintaining or fine tuning their performance. The interactive cycle becomes even more important to the supervisor as they take on the role of coach.

An employee demands certain requirements from their coach. The coach listens, questions, seeks clarification of what is expected of them and explores ways to measure performance. In many cases coach and employee enquire together for ways of exercising different methods to improve the employee's performance.

The employee puts new skills and ideas into practice, the coach observes, measures, gives feedback, supports, inspires and encourages the employee to achieve peak performance. There is an even balance of power between coach and employee in the learning process, albeit in this context that the coach has greater authority in their role as supervisor.

The contract between the coach and employee is very clear. There are three things that a supervisor needs to do with their employee to establish a contract:

1. Clarify with the employee the purpose of the coaching and what they aim to achieve. This clarification process involves focusing on the specific area for development.
2. Establish measures for assessment, benchmarks and time-scales.
3. Negotiate and clarify the support that the supervisor can provide the employee in the coaching process, i.e. information, observation, honest feedback without being too critical, encouragement, regular meetings, reading through written assignments, resources, etc. This nego-tiation is made in the context of other responsibilities both supervisor and employee have in their work.

Coaching others in their performance can be very satisfying work, especially where there is a good relationship between coach and employee.

Exercise 33 – Coaching skills assessment

Get your supervisors to rate themselves on a scale of 1 (not good) to 10 (very good) on the following coaching skills.

Skills assessment	Scale	Action to be taken
Empowering the employee	1 2 3 4 5 6 7 8 9 10	
Establishing purpose and aims	1 2 3 4 5 6 7 8 9 10	
Seeking clarification	1 2 3 4 5 6 7 8 9 10	
Establishing measures for assessment	1 2 3 4 5 6 7 8 9 10	
Setting benchmarks and timescales	1 2 3 4 5 6 7 8 9 10	
Observation skills	1 2 3 4 5 6 7 8 9 10	
Giving honest but not too critical feedback	1 2 3 4 5 6 7 8 9 10	
Giving encouragement	1 2 3 4 5 6 7 8 9 10	
Keeping to regular meetings	1 2 3 4 5 6 7 8 9 10	
Being realistic about fitting coaching into the wider workload	1 2 3 4 5 6 7 8 9 10	
Negotiating a contract	1 2 3 4 5 6 7 8 9 10	
Working interactively	1 2 3 4 5 6 7 8 9 10	

CONCLUSION

Training and coaching are two different types of learning that supervisors can engage in to achieve high performance in their staff. So it is true to say that supervisors will spend a lot of their time training and coaching staff. Developing their own skills to do this well will reflect in the learning of employees. Key to good skills in coaching and training is the ability to interact with staff throughout the learning process. Ultimately the essence of high performance lies in the freedom of staff to put their learning into action and to receive regular feedback.

CHAPTER 13

*F*OLLOWING THE LEADER

KEY LEARNING POINTS

- ■ Understand the notion of followership
- ■ Know how to develop and communicate a vision
- ■ Understand different kinds of power
- ■ Know how to release power in the workforce
- ■ Know how to use different styles of leadership in different situations

To lead effectively supervisors need to make positive use of power

WHAT IS LEADERSHIP?

Leading is the process of influencing other people to follow in the achievement of a common goal. No followers – no leader. There are many books on and different approaches to learning how to become a good leader. The approach I have taken here is simply to help supervisors begin their journey as leaders; learning how to induce followers.

Exercise 34 – Following the leader

I remember a game we used to play as children called 'Following the leader'. It was a game where we literally followed the elected leader and mimicked everything that they did. For the leader it felt powerful, having a sense of control over all these people following them; at school we could collect really long chains of followers around the playground. The more inspiring was the leader, the longer was the chain of followers. For the followers it was fun – as long as the leader was creative, inspiring, involving and didn't hog all the control for too long. Some of us always wanted a go at leading, others were happy to follow.

Leader games as children can teach us much about leader roles as adults, especially in pulling followers along with us.

Ask your supervisors to complete the following:

- Identify some managers inside and outside the organization that you admire for their leadership.
- What specific qualities make them a good leader?
- Name one or more of these leaders that you have followed, and maybe still do.
- What inspired you to follow?
- What can you learn from this experience in terms of becoming a leader yourself?

Discuss the answers in a group, paying particular attention to the attributes that inspire people to follow, for it is these that supervisors can learn from.

We will look at three different aspects of leadership that can invite followership:

A vision points in a direction, guiding people to a desired end point

- Vision and clarity of direction
- Integrity, that is, being true to held values and the organization's values
- Empowerment, that is, the ability to release the power in others.

THE VISION

A vision is seeing a picture of the future or having a strong sense of something that is possible. A vision describes what could be achieved in the future if certain actions were taken today.

A vision is not idealistic, it rests on a pragmatic knowledge of how things work. When I started writing this book I created a vision by asking myself, Who is this book for?, What is its purpose?, How will this book be used? In answering these questions I was able to clarify my vision, which helped me define the structure, content and style of my writing. So my vision wasn't just to write a book.

It may be that your supervisors are operating together towards a common departmental or organizational vision. That being the case, their task then is to communicate that vision to their staff and be clear as to how their area of responsibility will contribute to achieving the vision.

COMMUNICATING THE VISION

There are three important factors to communicating a vision well, that supervisors need to know about:

- Be clear and confident about the vision, with crisp use of language.
- Be open about aspects of the vision that are less clear to them, the supervisors.
- Make time available to discuss the implications of the vision with their staff and to explore how they could achieve the vision.

Communicating the vision well can inspire a sense of common purpose with people. Involving staff to define tasks and set goals that will achieve the vision will help gain their commitment.

Through this process people feel that what they do matters and that their efforts contribute to something worthwhile. They feel that they can affect the course of events.

People who feel important and involved feel powerful. That is what makes a visionary leader so valuable.

People who feel important and involved feel powerful

Exercise 35 – Following a vision

In Chapter 6 we explored briefly the importance of taking responsibility for ourselves; that a balanced lifestyle makes a difference to the way we are at work. We will use this notion for a visioning exercise for your supervisors. It will mean that they carry out the exercise outside of work practising through role play in the training session.

Get your supervisors to visualize, or get a sense of, something that they would like to do in the future with their family or friends. A vision that will add to the richness of their personal life. This may be an outing, a holiday, joining a sports club, winning a prize or event. The important thing is that it involves other people. Then get them to write their vision down as they would communicate it to the people involved.

Their next task is to communicate their vision. They can practise this with their peers as a role play (described below) or simply take it out of work to their family or friends. The idea is that once family and friends are 'pulled in' by the vision, it becomes a joint initiative rather than just one person's vision.

The task of the supervisor is then to make sure that the vision is kept in sight and achieved. For example:

I decided that I would like to be engaged in some activities with my teenage son before he left home for university. His main interests are football and cricket which don't really inspire me, so we never really end up doing things together.

My vision was to engage in an activity that we could do together and both enjoy. I told him this and he looked quite excited at the possibility, especially as he still had some choice in the matter. He asked a number of questions, wanting to clarify exactly what I had in mind, like a regular activity or a one-off event, and how much I was willing to pay. By way of example I suggested that perhaps we could join a scuba diving club which could end in a holiday where we go scuba diving, or simply visit a local outdoor centre where we could go pot holing or canoeing occasionally, or a trip to London where we could visit places that we would both be interested in and then go on to a show.

From our discussion we decided that we would like to expand our options so both agreed to make some enquiries, my son to phone some local centres and I would chase ideas farther afield.

What we had done was taken my vision and built on it together. Without the vision we would have continued in the same old familiar way, achieving nothing different. By having an open vision I 'pulled' my son in. If I had closed my vision down and said I would like us to spend a weekend together in London, I imagine he would have responded very reluctantly and unwillingly.

Get one supervisor to set up a role play, with the other supervisors playing the family members or friends involved in their vision. The supervisor then describes their vision.

Next, in their various roles, the other supervisors:

- Ask questions that seek clarification of the vision
- Contribute their ideas
- Agree goals that will achieve the vision and set SMART objectives
- Take responsibility for certain tasks.

Review the exercise paying particular attention to the supervisor's skills in:

- Clarity of vision
- Openness of vision
- Bringing family and friends 'into the vision'
- Leading discussion without controlling it
- Generating ideas
- Establishing resources
- Setting goals
- Setting objectives
- Delegation.

Your task as their manager will be to follow through the vision with each of your supervisors to see if they manage to achieve it. Taking this exercise seriously could achieve some fulfilling results for the people that you are working with.

RELEASING POWER

To lead effectively supervisors must make positive use of power, that is, their own power and the power of others. My own experience has consistently shown that when people get in touch with their power in a positive and valued way, their potential is readily harnessed into productive work and continual improvement.

There are two kinds of power: position power and personal power. Position power is derived from the formal authority given to supervisory and management roles. Components of position power include the power to reward or coerce employees, as well as the power to share or withhold information. The supervisor's power to coerce rests in the authority to discipline, give unsatisfactory performance reviews and withhold desired rewards. If people have experienced this kind of treatment in the past from their supervisors, the temptation can be to behave in a similar way. Yet the supervisor who is looking to achieve high results would do well to build on their power positively rather than negatively.

Some characteristics that enhance personal power include a clear vision, sense of mission, energy, moral force, strength of character, the ability to motivate and communicate, persuasiveness, self confidence, courage, extraversion, competence, integrity, honesty and charisma.

Exercise 36 – Differences in power

Here is an exercise for your supervisors to consider and then discuss.

List five managers or supervisors that you know quite well, making sure that they are a mix of those you respect highly and those you understand less well. Consider their behaviour, then answer the following questions:

1. How do they use their position power – is it positive, constructive, negative, coercive?
2. How do you respond to them?
3. How do others respond to them?
4. Do they have personal power and how do they choose to use it? Try to describe this clearly through the behaviours that they exhibit.
5. What impact does this have on their staff?
6. Do they help or hinder the organization's progress?
7. Who would you choose as a model for developing your own power?

RELEASING POWER THROUGH MOTIVATION

Motivation is the stimulus and energy that causes a person to act. It is not something that we give to people, but it is something that we can engender.

Motivation can be far more complex than we realize.

There are many life events, issues, social behaviours and so on that can undermine or depress positive energy. For example, you may have a worker who is totally committed to a job and then one day you notice that his enthusiasm seems to be declining. To utilize techniques that might restimulate his interest without finding out the cause of his mood change would be unwise. The chances are you would get it wrong. The answer is to talk to him and find out what is getting in the way. Then you might have some idea as to how you can help.

> Commitment to a shared vision can become the internal spark that ignites personal motivation

Trying to motivate people through force may lead to short-term benefits, but in the long term such behaviour evokes resentment and resistance making the leader's work much harder.

When supervisors foster motivation in employees they are leading and inspiring employees to apply energy to achieving organizational goals. For example, commitment to a shared vision can become the internal spark that ignites personal motivation. Reinforcement of motivation comes from frequent and spontaneous feedback, praise and appreciation.

'WALKING THE TALK'

Integrity is being true to one's own values and principles. Words used to describe people with integrity are sound, grounded, whole and honest.

Integrity can be achieved through self awareness. Self awareness helps people understand their values and the principles that are important to them. Self awareness also helps people understand how to get their needs met through open and honest contact with the world. The opposite to this is when people get their needs met through manipulating the environment underhandedly.

'Walking the talk' is the act of being true to the values of the organization. So, if the organization espouses values like 'open door management', the good leader leads by way of example, that is, by being approachable and meeting their staff through genuine interest and authenticity – not simply by leaving their office door open. Such integrity is the sign of a good leader.

People are attracted by integrity, they know where they stand and feel safe. Integrity in leaders is like holding a mirror up so that people can see their own integrity.

Acting with integrity releases personal power. It can feel risky because of feeling exposed, but the risk is worth it as long as the environment supports that process.

Exercise 37 – Acting with integrity

Get your supervisors to work in pairs and do the following exercise.

Say to each other, one at a time and swopping after each statement, 'Something I value is ...'. For example, *'Something that I value is confronting and dealing with difficulties that arise with colleagues, rather than avoiding them.'* Do not turn this into a conversation by trying to explain or seek clarification. The discipline of the exercise is important.

After about three minutes, continue the exercise and change the statement to 'A principle that I like to work with is ...'. For example, *'A principle that I like to work with is to speak to all of my staff before I start work in the morning.'*

Change again after three minutes, to 'I find it difficult to ...' (referring to values and principles that you find difficult to bring into your work). For example, *'I find it difficult to ask people senior to me to repeat what they are saying when I don't understand.'*

Staying in your pairs, spend a few minutes sharing what it was like to do the exercise.

LEADERSHIP STYLE

A good leader will be able to assess a given situation and adopt a style of leadership that will best achieve the results they are looking for. Well, that is the idea, but we are all human and usually rely on our own personal style of leadership, only changing when we are forced to through circumstance. Even so, knowing what is possible is a good starting point for supervisors. Establishing good habits now will reap benefits later.

We will concentrate here on three different styles of leadership and the position that each style adopts in leading teams and groups.

- Directive (leading from the front)
- Influential (leading from behind)
- Collaborative (leading from within).

Noticing people's responses to you and checking whether your style brings out the best in people is what is really important.

DIRECTIVE LEADERSHIP (LEADING FROM THE FRONT)

This approach maintains a high level of control and is a preferred style of operating for many leaders. It is based on the premise that the more control the leader has, the less others have. Overuse of directive power will lead to people feeling disempowered; the leader is denying the power of the workforce.

Being directive is telling people what to do, or giving direct information in a controlled environment. The times when directive leadership works at its best is in dealing with crisis, working with new recruits, teaching theory or sharing new information, operating in highly sensitive areas or where people's lives could be at risk and giving direction through times of change. When leaders are being directive it is absolutely clear who the leader is and who the followers are. Charismatic leadership is often based on a directive style, yet people are drawn to, and influenced by, the charisma of the leader. They reflect the power of the leader in their work.

Skilled directive leadership means behaving assertively rather than aggressively, imparting information with respect for the recipient's intelligence rather than patronizingly. It is also important for directive leaders to own their vulnerability and capacity to make mistakes.

INFLUENTIAL LEADERSHIP (LEADING FROM BEHIND)

Leading from behind means surrendering some control to staff, although not all. The leadership style is more subtle; the leader will intervene in the work of others in a way that encourages them in an appropriate direction. Employees will take up initiatives as though they thought of the idea themselves, albeit that the nudge came from the leader.

Influential leadership is like holding a container in which other people can release their personal power. They do not rely on the leader's power to achieve results, although they would notice if the leader stopped leading from behind. Holding the container is the leader's process of control. Leading takes the form of asking questions, revealing lack of knowledge in areas that staff know well and informing with integrity. The leader will influence through their personal power, their confidence and integrity, rather than their power of authority.

COLLABORATIVE LEADERSHIP (LEADING FROM WITHIN)

The role of the collaborative leader is quite subtle and incredibly inspiring for others when practised well. The key characteristic of this leadership style is the way in which the leader brings their presence into their work.

Presence is the presentation of a set of values and attitudes that a person has integrated well. The collaborative leader will model a way of working that is an expression of these values and attitudes, through a style that is authentic and engaging. People are often drawn to this style of leadership. There is usually mutual respect between the leader and employees; employees feel valued and recognized for their contribution.

I find that when I lead from within I regularly hear the people I am working with say or imply that 'we did it ourselves'. When they say this, it is a compliment to your collaborative style – it does nothing to boost your ego!

Collaborative leadership is *not* about giving up leadership responsibilities. It *is* a very empowering way to work as the leader relies on other people's personal power, capabilities, differences, knowledge and contribution to achieve the results they are looking for.

This way of leading can sometimes leave people feeling confused or uncertain. I have coached managers who were adamant that the only way to lead was through a collaborative approach, because they thought it was more humane. What they failed to see was that there are times when people genuinely need some direction before they can release themselves fully to a job, especially if they are used to a traditionally directive approach. It takes time to discover personal power when people have not had the opportunity to fully release it in the past.

Teamwork is ideal for a collaborative style of leadership. Achieving desired outcomes is the result of the leader's skill in communicating their vision and then deciding jointly with the team how to achieve that vision. The leader's success depends on their ability to build good teams, getting the team involved, working well together and taking joint responsibility for making decisions and for doing the work that has to be done.

Exercise 38 – Leadership style

Get your supervisors to consider what style of leadership they would use in the following situations.

Situation	Leadership style	Added comments and notes for your development
Developing a new initiative with the team		
Changing unproductive work procedures		
Implementing a new company policy		

Situation	Leadership style	Added comments and notes for your development
Pushing the staff to work with a philosophy of continual improvement		
Redirecting difficult behaviour with a member of staff		
Influencing your manager to resource a new initiative by your staff to improve work conditions		
Meeting with other supervisors to agree a new set of standards of practice for staff		
Presenting your ideas for a new work station to the board		
Holding your regular weekly review meeting with staff		
Interviewing for part-time administrative support		
Calling a meeting to deal with low health and safety standards in the workplace		

CONCLUSION

The best way for supervisors to start their journey of leadership is to think in terms of followership. The secret of this is to know which type of leadership to use in different situations. Styles of leadership are associated with different types of power, for instance the power of authority is stronger in directive leadership, whereas personal power, that is operating from a position of integrity, is associated more with collaborative styles of leadership. Either way, it is important to release the power within the workforce, in a positive and constructive way. In so doing, people feel good about their contribution, respecting and following their leader through to achieving their shared vision.

CHAPTER 14

WORKING WITH TEAMS

KEY LEARNING POINTS

- Understand the benefits of teamwork
- Be able to establish common purpose in a team
- Understand different patterns of communication
- Be able to engender good communication in a team
- Know how to brainstorm
- Understand the value of holding reviews
- Know how to encourage constructive feedback

TEAMS

Teams is a term used widely today for a group of people coming together for a common purpose. The benefit of teamwork is that people can achieve a lot more jointly than they could as a group of individuals.

A team may be a group of people who work closely together over a long period of time, supporting each other and relying on their different skills to achieve their goals. Or it may be a group of individuals whose only joint activity is to make decisions. Teams must be able to bring added value as a team to the department or business.

Cooperation is essential to team success; often leadership is shared, formal leadership being rotated among team members. Teamwork offers supervisors a good opportunity to bring out the informal leadership in staff; that is, encouraging people to take the lead on subjects they know well or to express viewpoints that they feel strongly about.

Supervisors can draw on teamwork in many ways. For example, for:

- Achieving results through joint effort
- Keeping projects aligned with the organization's vision
- Keeping staff well informed
- Problem solving, decision making and conflict resolution processes
- Nurturing creativity and inspiring motivation
- Selling new ideas
- Raising the profile of the department
- Developing networks to keep communication channels open and attract new business
- Supporting continuous improvement
- Encouraging continuous learning.

LEARNING TEAM SKILLS

The skill that a supervisor will need to develop will be their ability to bring a team together, that is, to work with the *team's process*. Many people do not achieve the best from their teams simply because they engage only with the content of discussion.

Working with the team process means developing the skill to flip from content to process at the flick of a switch. When the team is not achieving its objectives or doesn't seem to be working well, the chances are that the problem lies in the process not the content or tasks. Many teams go endlessly around in circles, concentrating on the content of their discussion, rather than looking at *how* they are working together.

Many teams go endlessly around in circles, concentrating on the content of their discussion, rather than looking at *how* they are working together

Scenario – The wasted meeting

The team met regularly once a week. They always had an agenda, which individual team members and the supervisor would contribute to between meetings as issues came up. The main purpose of the meetings seemed to be for making decisions, although no-one had really made this clear; this was an 'historical' team rather than a purposeful team.

It was 11 a.m. The supervisor, Andrew, had arrived early with copies of the agenda, as he always did. The five other members of the team were strolling down the corridor as though they had all the time in the world. By the time they had all made coffee and sat in their seats it was 11.15 a.m.

Andrew commented on the time, 'This meeting is supposed to start at 11 o'clock and I would prefer that we started on time in future.' A stunned silence fell in the room as Andrew rattled off the agenda. He then went back to the first item, 'New photocopier. Sandra, you were going to get some leaflets and costs. Have you managed to do that yet?' Sandra produced a pile of leaflets and the team started looking.

They all debated a few that seemed to stand out. It was nearing 11.30 a.m. and there were still several items on the agenda. The supervisor was getting agitated. 'I think it's time we made a decision and moved on. I would like us to buy the 500 L.' The team and Andrew went back into another ten-minute debate which was slowly developing into an argument between two members of the team.

Andrew called the meeting to a very quick end, asking Sandra to phone around some of the local traders to see if there were any special offers on photocopiers. He shifted all the other agenda items to the next meeting.

In this scenario the supervisor is getting caught up in the *what*, the decision-making process regarding the photocopier. He would have been much more successful had he intervened in the *how*, that is, the flow of interactions and behaviours.

Exercise 39 – A process intervention

Get your supervisors to read through the scenario and decide how many different ways they could have intervened in the process of the *how*, throughout the scenario. The list below will help.

Team process is:

- Working with purpose
- Problem-solving and decision-making methods
- Communication patterns
- Avoidance patterns
- Reviewing methods
- Feedback styles
- Establishing a learning philosophy
- Taking joint responsibility for the life of the team
- Awareness and acceptance of difference.

Then get your supervisors to role play the scenario with someone taking the role of Andrew, experimenting with different ways to intervene in the process. It will be useful for the team to notice the difference to them, between a content and a process intervention.

When the exercise is complete, step out of role and discuss what you learned from the exercise.

The cycle of effective working practices is all about process. Figure 14.1 shows the phases in the team process.

PHASE 1 – ESTABLISHING PURPOSE

Establishing the purpose of a team is extremely important. The purpose of the team has to support the individual needs of the team as well. If it doesn't, the team will be short lived or exist in name only. When I am asked to develop teams who are not working well together, I always start by asking individuals, 'What's in it for you belonging to this team?' I then ask, 'What can you as a team achieve that you otherwise could not achieve as individuals?' These two questions invariably lead to clarifying the purpose of the team, as well as raising the team spirit.

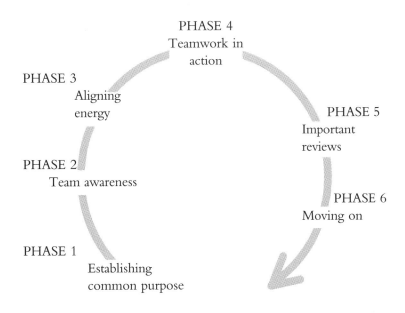

FIGURE 14.1: Managing the team process

Teams who meet without appreciating the full value of the team, could end up 'going through the motions' of team meetings; following agendas, but never really feeling fulfilled by the 'weekly' event.

The trap is going to meetings through habit rather than purposeful intent.

What can you as a team achieve that you otherwise could not achieve as individuals?

PHASE 2 – TEAM AWARENESS

Teams work better together if people are able to engage well with each other at a personal level. To do this they have to step out of cliché speak and away from their role jargon to engage at a more personal level, as shown in Figure 14.2. People keep to cliché speak and role jargon out of habit or they imagine it is threatening to bring themselves as human beings into a meeting. Important things are not said or heard, people consequently make assumptions and bring their prejudices in to the meeting. Cleaning up this interchange is the task of the supervisor. Once achieved, the team have the capacity to work with a learning philosophy.

The trap is for a team to rush into action before they are ready and communicating well together.

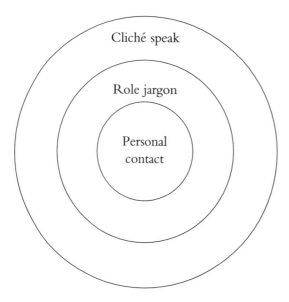

FIGURE 14.2: Levels of contact in teams

Here are three useful pointers that will help supervisors encourage good communication at a personal level in their team. All of them are related to tactics that people use to avoid human contact and are typical patterns in cliché speak and role jargon.

'TALKING ABOUT' OR INTELLECTUALIZING

When the team get sidetracked into 'talking about' or intellectualizing, bring them back on track to the real issue that they have moved away from.

DE-PERSONALIZED LANGUAGE

There are times when people use 'we', 'one', 'it', 'you' when they really mean 'I'. In so doing they manage to make statements usefully vague, which is safer than taking personal responsibility for what they are saying. This is a good tactic for avoiding contact. A useful intervention would be, 'Trevor, I notice that you said "we" when you complained about the food. I'm not sure that everyone agrees with you.' This way it leaves Trevor to either check out his statement with the team or take full responsibility for what he is saying.

SPEAKING INTO THE AIR

Talking into the centre of the table or carpet is a good way to avoid contact with the team, or to specific people. For example:

Vicki	(A team member, looking at the centre of the table) Some people around here seem to think that it would be a waste of resources developing this computer programme.
Supervisor	Who in the team do you believe thinks this?
Vicki	I don't know, but I am getting some bad vibes.
Supervisor	I suggest you look around the team and when you see someone who you imagine is not supportive of developing the programme, ask them.

Vicki looked at each member of the team one by one. Selecting two members, she asked them their views and was able to ascertain their specific reasons for not fully supporting the programme. This led to a slight change of plan and Vicki went ahead with the full support of the team.

Exercise 40 – Avoidance patterns

Get your supervisors to list as many cliché statements as they can that they hear around them in the workplace. Ask them what impact these cliché statements have on them. Have some fun and get them to try some out on each other.

Then get your supervisors to do the same with role jargon. What patterns of language exist with supervisors, managers and departmental staff?

Discuss with them how they might change the way they communicate with each other and their staff. Ask them what difficulties they think they might have.

The point being made about clichés and role jargon is not that they are wrong but that they are used as an avoidance of contact with people. Clichés and role jargon will always do this. Awareness of ourselves helps us to decide whether this type of language is appropriate for the situation we are in.

VALUING DIFFERENCE

Many people enjoy teamwork, it provides them with a sense of belonging in a small community – a basic human need. Such an environment offers the ideal opportunity to discover difference. Without feeling a sense of belonging, many people will be reluctant to show their difference for fear of rejection and isolation.

In particular, supervisors will be faced with drawing on individual potential, and integrating differences like different ways of thinking, personality styles and patterns of behaviour. Other differences they may be faced with are race, colour, national origin, culture, language, religion, gender, sexual preference, age and physical or mental disability. Dealing with prejudices and myths relating to apparent differences like these are some of the challenges that supervisors will face. The task for the supervisors will be to encourage everyone in the team to respect and tolerate difference, owning their prejudices and surfacing misunderstandings.

Supervisors can take the following steps to bridge difference:

- Address people directly.
- Lead by example. Treat all people with dignity and respect.
- Allow themselves to be fascinated by people's uniqueness. This way they can draw on and utilize each individual's special contribution.
- To prevent misunderstandings use simple language, explain clearly and ask employees for clarification when they do not fully understand what they are trying to say.
- To mediate when conflicts arise between employees, learn about different cultures, values, beliefs and differences in terminology, drawing on their problem-solving and conflict management skills.

The purpose of Phases 2 and 3 in teamwork is to bring the team in line with each other. If a team moves too quickly into action important issues get missed and outcomes are not achieved well.

> Many people enjoy teamwork, it provides them with a sense of belonging

TEAM RESPONSIBILITY

A small but significant step to take with teams is to ensure shared responsibility for the life of the team beyond team meetings. By this I mean that each member takes a shared responsibility to ensure that the team is kept going, that it doesn't just exist for 30 minutes a week at the team meeting, but is constant. If responsibility for the life of the team always falls back on the leader, the commitment in the team will drop and the leader will feel burdened.

PHASE 3 – ALIGNING ENERGY

The energy of the team is the spirit and enthusiasm that emerges from working together

The energy of the team is the spirit and enthusiasm that emerges from working together. Even when the going gets tough this spirit exists. Teams engage in problem solving and decision making leading to action. This is not only to support the team objective but also to provide support during problems and difficulties that individual team members face.

Phase 3 is a very creative part of the cycle. Using brainstorming and decision-making techniques to engage with the creativity in the team can be fun and highly beneficial; closing down options too soon could deny the team potential that exists. Involving all members of the team reinforces feelings of value in the teamwork.

BRAINSTORMING

Brainstorming is a process for surfacing and expanding on ideas without censoring. Brainstorming in a team enables team members to build on each other's ideas. Brainstorming involves the following steps:

1. Articulate an issue or problem.
2. Team members offer their ideas for ways of dealing with the issue or managing the problem:
   - Do not censure
   - Do not discuss or criticize
   - Encourage the wildest ideas
   - Build on other people's ideas
   - Think laterally
   As people declare their ideas write them down on a flip chart.

3. Get the team to vote on what they think are the most creative suggestions for solving the problem. Each member has three votes. It can be fun to use small stickers for people to place on the flip chart beside their chosen suggestions.

4. The problem owner then takes these suggestions away and acts on them.

When team members feel supported in their problems and idea generation they will value the support that good teamwork engenders.

PHASE 4 – TEAMWORK IN ACTION

The process part of this phase is in the team working together rather than individually. A good analogy is to consider a sports team. The football team, badminton team, rugby team, cricket team, hockey team, all play to each other's strengths; not as groups of individuals. Even when members of a team are not together there is still a sense of working as part of a team.

Sports teams play to each other's strengths; not as groups of individuals

The supervisor can play a key role in this phase to ensure team spirit continues and that people do not become isolated, encouraging individuals to take responsibility for their teamness, keeping in touch with their colleagues and the task being undertaken. The team should be supporting each other when things go wrong, giving feedback and encouraging continued learning.

PHASE 5 – THE IMPORTANCE OF REVIEWS

In busy environments, especially when teams seem to be firefighting all the time, reviews become rushed or missed altogether. The sad thing is that teams fail to recognize how reviews could help them step out of the firefighting into a more pro-active and fulfilling process.

Encourage your supervisors to always hold their reviews – and to know that they will gain benefit from this. There are four things that they need to ensure this happens:

- To celebrate and gain satisfaction from actions taken
- To give recognition and feedback to each other

If you believe you failed then you didn't hear the feedback

- To learn and improve, or change the way the work is done
- To assess how the team is working together; this keeps the team aligned and enables continued improvement in the way teams work together.

CELEBRATION

Getting the team to recognize their achievements, even if these were very small, reinforces a sense of value and self worth. Going straight into criticizing and picking to pieces the work that has been done, loses the satisfaction that we all need to gain from the hard work that we put in.

Leaping from task to task will miss this part of the cycle out completely. Without satisfaction people become disheartened, morale drops and the work will suffer.

FEEDBACK

Encourage team members to give each other good constructive feedback. When negative feedback is being given, a good rule of thumb is to give feedback that the other person can act on and then to support their learning from it. Opinionated and subjective feedback can rarely be acted on and frequently leads to defensiveness and difficult relations. For example, if someone said to you, 'You're talking a load of rubbish,' you probably would shut up and distance yourself from that person.

A better way of putting it would be, 'You seem to be contradicting yourself, do you mean X or Y?' That enables you to clarify the content of your discussion or even acknowledge your own confusion in the matter.

One of the tasks of the supervisor in their teams is to encourage specific feedback, intervening when unhelpful feedback is given. The following scenario elaborates on this.

Scenario – Giving feedback

The team are holding a review after not meeting the deadline on a proposal for a contract. They are five minutes into their review and the energy is low.

Tom I thought you did a lousy job on that report, Sally.

Sally feels hurt and angry. She has put hours into the report; nobody has offered any help and she has battled on in the best way she knew how.
    Gill, the supervisor, notices Sally's glare at Tom.

Gill   It might be more helpful for Sally if you tell her what you thought wasn't good about her report and how you think she could change it.

Tom fidgets in his seat. He has not expected to have to be that specific. His anger is really about missing the deadline. The contract would have been such an exciting one for him. Sally has let him down by spending so long on putting the report together.

Tom   It was far too long, putting that much detail in it wasn't necessary.

Sally Well, Tom, if it was so important to you why didn't you offer to help? You knew I was struggling.

Tom   You said you wanted to do it.

Sally flicks her red hair away from her face and looks Tom in the eye.

Sally Saying I want to do it doesn't mean that I don't want help. I asked you several times, each time you told me to get on with it myself, you were too busy.

Tom   I'm sorry, Sally, you're right. I feel really disappointed about losing the contract. I could have helped you. The report was well written but I

> think you put too much detail in it. You could have been more concise and cut the report down by a third.
>
> **Sally** Would you be willing to go through it with me to look at how I could have improved it?
>
> Tom agrees and the meeting moves on.

PHASE 6 – INTEGRATING LEARNING AND MOVING ON

This is the phase of taking in what has been achieved, integrating what has been learned and creating space to move on to the next project.

When large, long-term projects reach their end, project teams often feel a sense of emptiness and want to look for things to fill the space quickly. This can be a useful time to take stock of how well the team are working, looking at the balance between work and personal life and allowing new things to emerge in their own time, without pushing forward too quickly.

Endings are an important time for ensuring continuity of what really matters.

Exercise 41 – Skills assessment for running effective teams

Get your supervisors to assess themselves on a scale of 1 (not good) to 10 (very good) on the following team skills. Then select three skills that they would like to develop more and decide how they will do this.

Team skill	Rating	Action to be taken
Establishing common purpose	1 2 3 4 5 6 7 8 9 10	
Identifying what individual team members need from the team	1 2 3 4 5 6 7 8 9 10	
Balancing discussion content with watching the process	1 2 3 4 5 6 7 8 9 10	
Encouraging good contact	1 2 3 4 5 6 7 8 9 10	
Building an environment for learning	1 2 3 4 5 6 7 8 9 10	
Letting go of responsibility for the life of the team	1 2 3 4 5 6 7 8 9 10	
Using clear concise language	1 2 3 4 5 6 7 8 9 10	
Valuing difference	1 2 3 4 5 6 7 8 9 10	
Drawing out difference in the team	1 2 3 4 5 6 7 8 9 10	
Aligning the energy of the team	1 2 3 4 5 6 7 8 9 10	
Celebrating achievements	1 2 3 4 5 6 7 8 9 10	
Giving helpful feedback	1 2 3 4 5 6 7 8 9 10	

CONCLUSION

Getting results out of teams is an art, and even with the best of skills if the team do not have purpose there will be no results, only people going through the motions.

There are many approaches to teamwork. The approach here has been to help supervisors understand how to work with the interactive process of team members. In so doing they will develop a good communication style, and good contact, even though this might be challenging at times. Any future learning that your supervisors do in relation to working with teams will be supported by the skills and understanding gained now.

CHAPTER 15

WORKING TOGETHER

KEY LEARNING POINTS

■ For you and your supervisor to be able to align yourselves with each other in your work roles

■ For you and your supervisor to be able to 'tune in' to each other as people

■ For you and your supervisor to know how to maintain a good working relationship

HOW CAN YOU AND YOUR SUPERVISORS ADD VALUE BY WORKING TOGETHER?

Many managers choose supervisors on the basis of their competence and their loyalty. These two factors are key to the success of the managers and, of course, the subsequent success of the supervisors. It isn't that other people particularly notice competence and loyalty; they notice results. They will, however, notice and judge lack of competence and lack of loyalty. This will have a negative effect on the reputation of the managers and the department.

One of the most important aspects of a supervisor's job is

to understand how they can support you, their manager; how they can help you succeed and perform even better. In return they have your support in their professional development, the challenges they take on and in their learning. Your success and their success become entwined in a mutual exchange. This mutual exchange can lead to achieving more than if you and your supervisor work independently of each other and adds value to the work that you do.

BECOMING ALIGNED

In Chapter 3 your supervisors developed a management chart to understand the part their role played in the management system of the organization. The task now is to focus in on your role as manager in relation to them in their role as supervisors.

Exercise 42 – Becoming aligned

One way of achieving this is to invite your supervisors to an open enquiry session with you to discuss your work. There may be very specific aspects of your responsibilities that you want them to know about. They may have questions that they want to ask which you hadn't considered. Invite them to write down their questions before the session. This will provide a basis to start and build upon discussion.

The following are some key points to include:

- The purpose of your meeting, explaining how you can add value to the achievements of the department by working together.
- Explain more about your vision.
- Describe your goals and objectives.
- Define measures of success.
- Your key areas of responsibility.
- The demands that others place on you.
- The constraints on resources that are put on you. Even though you may not always be able to give supervisors what they want, they need to know what informs your decisions.
- How you can help each other succeed.

Review your discussion with your supervisors by way of completing. How was it for them? How was it for you?

DECISION MAKING

Supervisors need to clarify how much authority and scope they have in decision making, and what you, their manager, expect of them. This clarity can only be gained through discussion and negotiation. Where the agreement is unclear the supervisor must either seek clarification, or alternatively refer decision making to you.

Even when supervisors are absolutely clear about the level of their authority, it will help their relationship with you to discuss decisions that they have made. Naturally all decisions must be aligned with your goals and vision.

BECOMING ATTUNED

BUILDING THE RELATIONSHIP

The next thing to focus on is how you and your supervisors can build a good working relationship together. You will achieve more if you have a trusting relationship, a clear understanding of your expectations of each other and a willingness for both of you to take responsibility for the maintenance of the relationship. You can do this, allowing your humanness to shine through your work roles.

BUILDING TRUST THROUGH OPENNESS AND INTEGRITY

Trust is not a skill to be developed. It is a quality in a relationship that is earned and it emerges through being open, honest and acting with integrity. Some exercises were provided in Chapter 13 to help supervisors to understand and appreciate their own values, which are characteristic of integrity. Openness and honesty with others starts with being open and honest with ourselves. The opposite is being manipulative and calculating in order to get our needs met, or blaming others for the mistakes that we make ourselves. By being open and honest with ourselves we build trust with others.

Trust is not a skill to be developed; it is a quality in a relationship that is earned

Acting with integrity was
described as a leadership
quality in Chapter 13

Trust is also gained through sharing confidences. Here is an exercise that you can do with your supervisors that will help build trust.

Exercise 43 – Trust building

This exercise is about sharing information about yourselves that you might consider to be risky.

Share something with your manager/supervisors/peers that feels a bit risky. Before you share this, assess what you will share on a risk scale from 1 (low risk) to 10 (high risk). Although risk assessment in this context is very subjective and therefore should not be assessed against those of others, the following is a general guide.

Risk level 1 'I feel concerned that the senior managers in this organization do not value and support initiative.'
Risk level 5 'I really put my foot in it last week when I talked to my team about the new policy on travelling expenses. I forgot that Toyin has a different arrangement from everyone else. She will lose out badly. She was quite upset. I was embarrassed that I had made such a blunder.'
Risk level 9 'I have just taken up lessons in South African dancing with drums. I wasn't going to tell you because I thought you would all laugh.'

When people share their risks do not allow discussion to develop, just listen and acknowledge what you heard.

Taking risks in sharing confidences can be a useful little exercise to do on a regular basis. You could work your way up from 1 to 10 or simply let people find their own level of risk taking.

DECLARING EXPECTATIONS

Many relationships fail to
work well because
expectations are not made
clear

Many relationships fail to work well because expectations are not made clear. This is a bit like having a dot-to-dot drawing. In order to see the picture clearly we have to connect the dots. If we don't do this, we have to guess what the picture is by looking for clues. We are likely to guess partly (or completely) wrong because we are guessing according to our own life experiences, not tuning into the other person's life experiences. In the view that no two people ever have the same perceptions of life, acting on guesswork is not likely to achieve productive end results.

Exercise 44 – Sharing expectations

This is an exercise that opens up expectations between yourself and your supervisors. Include yourself in the exercise.

Each person takes a turn, going around to everyone present and saying, 'In my work what I expect from you is ...'. There may be a number of expectations for one person and just one or two for others. After each round allow one minute for clarification questions only. Then someone else can have a turn.

When everyone has had a go open up the group for discussion to challenge some of the expectations that have emerged.

This exercise can be excellent as long as you are rigorous in maintaining the structure and not opening debate too soon.

MAINTAINING THE RELATIONSHIP

VALUING YOUR DIFFERENCE

We discussed in Chapter 14 the value of understanding and respecting difference in teams. Now we are saying that the same principles apply between you and your supervisors.

We are all different in so many ways, usually more so than we are similar. Understanding these differences, by allowing people to stand out and be valued for their individuality, can lead to much greater opportunities than if everyone is perceived as similar. You and your supervisors will all be different in many ways. If you look, you can discover your differences as you work together day to day. Regard these differences when they surface as finding nuggets of gold. They are of great value to you all.

Regard these differences when they surface as finding nuggets of gold

UNDERSTANDING EACH OTHER'S STRENGTHS AND WEAKNESSES

Strengths in the workplace are frequently associated with competencies, that is, competencies related to the job. Rarely are people invited to share their hidden talents. They keep them to themselves as though they are not important. Yet it is these talents that a business can draw on to add value to their work. For example, fluency in languages can be a hidden talent of great benefit to an organization in today's world where international boundaries are crossing. Musical talent is another example that reflects an ability to persevere with learning and of good co-ordination. So it could pay to take time discovering the hidden talents of your supervisors and acknowledging your own to them.

To share each other's weaknesses means understanding ourselves and owning that we are different. Weaknesses are differences and only become weaknesses in context. They are different patterns of behaviour that achieve different end results. To know that there are some things that we are really not very good at, that is, we have patterns that don't achieve the results that we are looking for, will open up the possibility of exploring other ways of achieving these results. A good example of this can be found in the use of computers. Some people will spend hours formatting their desk top publishing documents to a fine quality, whereas others are concerned that the content is good but will keep the formatting to a minimum. These differences could produce high quality work if they are brought together, if people recognize that their own weaknesses are the other person's strengths.

Owning weaknesses can lead to discovering and building on other people's strengths. After all, strengths and weaknesses are only labels that we put on differences.

Weaknesses are differences, and only become weaknesses in context

Strengths and weaknesses are only labels that we put on differences

Exercise 39 — Strengths and weaknesses

Working with your supervisors do the following exercise.

Spend some time (this could be between meetings) considering what you believe to be your hidden strengths and weaknesses.

Strengths

Think of how you spend your personal life. Write down a list of your hobbies, the tasks you are involved in at home, the committees you belong to, the voluntary work that you do.

Having done this consider the strengths and skills that you

have developed through each activity. If you are struggling with this, imagine someone else is engaged in that activity and identify the strengths that they exhibit. Then consider if you have these strengths as well.

How might these strengths be useful in your work?

Weaknesses

Notice the patterns of behaviour in your life.

- The way you like to live and organize your life.
- What you like to do, what you don't like to do.
- What you know about, what you don't know about.
- What you would like to learn to do, what you will never be interested in doing.

Then answer the following questions:

1. In the context of your work how might your patterns of behaviour be seen as weaknesses?
2. Is there anything you can do to change this pattern?
3. Is there a mutual exchange that you can organize with your manager, peers and staff to overcome this weakness, ensuring that end results are not diminished?

Once everyone has done this exercise for themselves, allow time for sharing in a learning group session together.

MAINTAINING LOYALTY

We discussed in Chapter 4 issues around split loyalties between staff (operational peers and colleagues) and management. Your role as the manager is to ensure that the loyalty from your supervisors is sustained. You will manage this by supporting supervisors:

- In managing conflicts
- In their career development
- In their success and achievements in their work
- by keeping strong disagreements private.

MAINTAINING RELATIONSHIPS

Set time aside every week when you can meet with your supervisors for 'maintenance work' on your relationships. This needs to be unpressured time where you can engage in good, open, honest communication.

CONCLUSION

Building your capacity to become aligned and attuned is the path to success in the way you and your supervisors work together. This task cannot be left to fate, it requires determined effort and continued maintenance. It is a process of learning and discovery. The benefits will be felt by you in your work and in your success as a manager; by staff in their confidence in you; your supervisors working as a team; and the organization in the added value that together you bring.

INDEX

Also from McGraw-Hill

79 / 80 Things You Must Do to be a Great Boss
David Freemantle

'One of my favourite handbooks.'
Kevin Keegan, Manager,
Newcastle United Football Club.
*For managers aiming to get the best out
of their people, this book is a must!*

ISBN: 0 07 709043 8
£12.95

Developing a Learning Culture
Sue Jones

*"A highly practical book that should be read by all managers and
trainers who are concerned with implementing change, strategies
and collaborative teamworking."* Management Training.

ISBN: 0 07 707983 3
£19.95

101 Ways to Develop Your People Without Really Trying
Peter Honey

*Thousands of ideas on how to fit piggyback learning and
development on the shoulders of normal work activities.*

ISBN: 0 07 709183 3
£16.95

Dealing With People Problems at Work
Steven Palmer and Tim Burton

*'A down-to-earth guide for managers in how to handle a range
of everyday people problems found in most work situations.
This book's practical step-by-step approach will help many who
find their work colleagues a palpable source of job stress."*
Gary Cooper, Manchester School of Management.

ISBN: 0 07 709177 9
£12.95

A Manager's Guide to Self-Development, Third Edition
Mike Pedler

*This working philosophy of
self-development has become the
indispensable guide to helping managers
realise their potential and improve their
abilities and performance.*

ISBN: 0 07 707829 2
£14.95

Developing Managers as Coaches
Frank S. Salisbury

*Based on the view that everyone has a "seed of greatness",
this book will inspire you to leap forward into the crucial concept
of coaching in the business environment.*

ISBN: 0 07 707892 6
19.95

The Power of Personal Influence
Richard Hale

*"A most valuable book which provides a refreshingly practical
approach to improving all aspects of how we influence others."*
Wenche Marshall Foster, Chief Executive, Perrier Group.

ISBN: 0 07 709131 0
£14.95

Vision At Work
John Mitchell

*Highlighting the link between strategy
and the decision-making process, this
book explores how creative leaders can
translate 'vision' into effective 'action'.*

ISBN: 0 07 709085 3
£19.95

Workplace Counselling
Di Kamp

*"Di Kamp is able to describe ways to bring out the best in people.
All that remains now is for the rest of us to implement the ideas."*
Rob Ball, Rover Group Ltd.

ISBN: 0 07 709152 3
£19.95

The Project Manager as Change Agent
J Rodney Turner

*"This text is required reading for all those involved and
interested in the management of change in the 90s."*
Eric Gabriel, Vice-President, Association of Project Managers.

ISBN: 0 07 707741 5
£24.95

The Handbook of Project-Based Management
J Rodney Turner

*A radical re-evaluation of the often overlooked role of the project
manager who has to maximise strategic and successful change.*

ISBN: 0 07 707656 7
£45.00

Prices are correct at the time of going to press but are subject to change

Available from all good bookshops

McGraw-Hill Publishing Company
Shoppenhangers Road, Maidenhead, Berkshire, SL6 2QL, England
Tel: ++44 (0) 1628 23431 / Fax: ++44 (0) 1628 35895